Where Are the Customers' Yachts?

Wiley Investment Classics

Reminiscences of a Stock Operator
  Edwin Lefèvre

Where Are the Customers' Yachts?
or   A Good Hard Look at Wall Street
  Fred Schwed, Jr.

Where Are the Customers' Yachts?

or
A Good Hard Look
at Wall Street

FRED SCHWED, JR.
Illustrated by Peter Arno

JOHN WILEY & SONS, INC.
New York · Chichester · Brisbane
Toronto · Singapore

Copyright © 1940, 1955, 1995 by Fred Schwed, Jr.
Foreword © 1995 by John Wiley & Sons, Inc.
Published by John Wiley & Sons, Inc.
Originally published in 1940 by Simon & Schuster.

Library of Congress Cataloging-in-Publication Data:

Schwed, Fred, 1901 or 2–1966.
    Where are the customers' yachts?, or, A good hard look at Wall
Street / Fred Schwed, Jr.
       p. cm. — (Wiley investment classics)
    Originally published: New York : Simon and Schuster, 1940.
    ISBN 0-471-11979-2.—ISBN 0-471-11978-4 (paper)
    1. Wall Street. 2. Stocks. 3. Investment. 4. Wall Street—
Humor. 5. Stocks—Humor. 6. Investments—Humor. 7. Wall
street—Caricatures and cartoons. I. Title. II. Title: Good hard
look at Wall Street. III. Series.
HG4572.S35 1994
332.64'273—dc20
                                   94-40815

Printed in the United States of America
10 9 8 7 6 5 4 3 2 1

FOR JACK

The author and the publishers
of WHERE ARE THE CUSTOMERS' YACHTS? *are*
grateful to the editors of The Fcrum *for*
permission to reproduce certain passages that
appeared originally in that magazine.

"*The information contained herein,
while not guaranteed by us, has been obtained
from sources which have not in the past proved
particularly reliable.*"

Foreword

I like to think that when I first stumbled across this delightful little book the ghost of its author stumbled right along with me, with a gin and tonic in his hand. I had been leafing idly through the Princeton University library collection and had pretty well concluded that there was nothing written about Wall Street in the 1920s of use to someone hoping to write a book about Wall Street in the 1980s. But as I replaced the final dusty volume on the shelf I noticed beside it another, more luridly titled, more tastefully bound. And once I picked it up I did not put it down until I had finished.

Long before Burton Malkiel wrote *A Random Walk Down Wall Street*, Fred Schwed, Junior, actually took one. He went to work on Wall Street in the early 1920s after being ejected from Princeton at the end of his senior year—for having a girl in his room at six o'clock in the evening. He stayed only a couple of years and wrote only this one book about the experience. But it is a gem. It was a funny book about Wall Street that is still a funny book about Wall Street. It continues to amuse us while so much of the other "humorous" writing of the period now seems hokey and obscure. It endures mainly, I think, because it is still relevant to our experience.

What Schwed has done is capture fully—in deceptively simple language—the lunacy at the heart of the investment business: the widely held belief that there is someone out there who can tell you how to turn a little money into a lot, quickly. If there is a guiding principle in what follows it is that "the subject of choosing profitable investments does not lend itself to competence. There is almost no visible supply." And yet many people give investment advice and more receive it. What should we make of their activity?

Having seen the business of investing first hand, Fred Schwed decided that he was far more amused than outraged. "The broker influences the customer with his knowledge of the future," he wrote, "but only after he has convinced himself. The worst that should be said of him is that he wants to convince *himself* badly and that he therefore succeeds in convincing himself—generally badly."

That Schwed chose not sin but folly as his subject probably had as much to do with his temperament as it did with Wall Street. He was the son of a short seller who went bankrupt in the bull market of the 1920s. He lived most of his adult life in Rowayton, Connecticut, which he called "the Athens of South Norwalk." He preferred golf and drinking to work and wrote only a few things, of which the best known today is a children's book called *Wacky the Small Boy*. His obituary in the *New York Times*, in 1960, drew upon a self-portrait he had penned for a dust jacket: "One hundred and eighty two pounds formerly; curly brown hair in many photographs taken before WWII; owe

xi

everything to my mother and small amounts to others; am fond of good clean fun if anyone can suggest good clean fun that does not cause shortness of breath.''

He must have enjoyed his own book.

MICHAEL LEWIS

Contents

CONTENTS

ONCE IN THE DEAR dead days beyond recall, an out-of-town visitor was being shown the wonders of the New York financial district. When the party arrived at the Battery, one of his guides indicated some handsome ships riding at anchor. He said,

"Look, those are the bankers' and brokers' yachts."

"Where are the customers' yachts?" asked the naïve visitor.

—Ancient story

Introduction
to the 1955 Bull Market Edition

THIS BOOK FIRST AP-
peared fifteen years ago, when conditions in the
financial markets were different from what they are
today, and so were the conditions in the author. *Plus
ça change, plus c'est la même chose,* as the French
say. Never, more than now, have I wondered just
what that means.

Not many books are remembered after fifteen
years, but of the people who had any interest in
Wall Street in 1940, I happen to know that a good
many of them can recall this one. Not all these
people bought,* or read the book, or even glanced
at Mr. Arno's cartoons. In my travels I have found

---

* This is easily the most reliable statement in the new edition,
and can be documented.

that the number of people who know of this book, but have never happened to purchase a copy, is remarkable. In all this time, rarely has no eye lighted up when I casually rammed *Where Are the Customers' Yachts?* into the conversation.

This immortality is all attributable to just five words out of a 40,000-word text—the five words of that title. It is fitting that at this time I divulge the wellsprings of my inspiration concerning it:

The little story from which it derives is printed on the page preceding this one. I had heard the gag shortly after getting my first job in the Street, in 1927. So did everyone else who ever got such a job. It lay buried in my subconscious for a dozen years. After all, it is not the sort of story that can be told in mixed company, because everyone in mixed company has heard it before. Then I included it somewhere in my first draft of manuscript. My editor, Mr. Jack Goodman, wrenched it out of there and stuck it on the book's spine. I recall I objected violently but to no avail, as usual. I had recently learned from my brother, an expert on copyright law, that a title cannot be copyrighted. Thus I had planned to have my book appear under a good title, *The Adventures of Huckleberry Finn.*

Soon after the book was published and generously advertised I received a flattering amount of mail from old Wall Street hands, calling me a plagiarist. One of them, however, was courteous about it, and competent too. This elderly gentleman had taken the trouble to send along a photostat of a periodical called *The Tattler,* published in San Francisco, in the year of my birth. The remark had been murmured, I read with fascination, by a Mr. Travis, a wit who was then only less famed than Wilson Mizner. I learned that Mr. Travis had a slight stammer, which made more engaging what he had to say on a cold windy day while shivering next to the Aquarium. With proper scholarship the title should have been *Where Are the C-C-Customers' Yachts?*

One thing is clear to me: the joke I selected to swipe had merit from the start. Jokes with less merit do not live on for half a century, with or without my assistance.

My favorite review of the book (indeed my favorite review of any book by anybody) was supplied by Frank Sullivan. I was not acquainted with Mr. Sullivan, then or now, but his review caused us two economists to have a brief correspondence. In his review he wrote in part:

> "[Mr. Schwed] thinks Wall Streeters are incurable romantics and children at heart. Well, aren't we all? I suppose I was an adult that day in 1937 when I bought Pennsylvania Railroad at 40. . . .
>
> " . . . Wall Street could probably do with a lot more such antic philosophers. If I were J. P. Morgan, and I have no reason to suspect that I am not, I would invite Fred Schwed, Jr., to become a partner forthwith."

So I sat down and wrote thoughtfully to Frank Sullivan, care of the *New York Herald Tribune* Books.

"MY DEAR MR. SULLIVAN,

I thank you for your excellent review of my recent book. However, the matter I wish to take up with you as soon as possible is not a literary matter at all.

"I was deeply interested in the part where you said that

if you were Mr. J. P. Morgan, you would invite me to
become your partner, and you indicated that there was far
more than a possibility that you were actually Mr. Morgan.

"I will be frank with you. Where I happen to be em-
ployed now business is not quite so hot as could be desired.
A Morgan partnership could be construed as a distinct
improvement, or at least an upward step, in my career.
Thus I find that *my* future is inextricably bound up with
your identity.

"I would like you to go over yourself carefully and determine once and for all if you're Morgan the wonderful
financier, or still just Sullivan, the wonderful comical
writer. Of course if it turns out that you haven't got a big
black mustache, all our dreams come tumbling down.

"If you can help me in this I have a return proposition
to offer *you*. If, at any time in the future, it turns out that
I am Mrs. Ogden Reid, I will hire you as chief editorial
writer of the *New York Herald Tribune,* at any salary
which you care to name. That is, of course, any salary
within reason, as you no doubt understand.

Sincerely, etc."

I promptly got back a reply from, alas, Sullivan,
who, as it turned out, he actually was. The letter
was sharply disappointing and I threw it away. But

I remember to this day his main point. He politely wrote that to require me to become Mrs. Ogden Reid would be asking for too much effort on my part. However, if I would just do something simpler and put Pennsylvania RR common back to 40 he would be eternally grateful.

It was but the work of a moment to get a quote on Pennsy. It was at that time 11¼–½. I felt a chill of discouragement sweep over me, and I said to myself, "Ah, the heck with it!"

As I write this in the spring of '55 I note that I seem to be pushing it back to 40 for him.

When it was first suggested that this year would be a proper occasion to get out a new edition, I craftily thought to myself: yes, and I will reread my book carefully and gently remold such opinions as have not entirely withstood the acid test of time—a whole fifteen years of it. But after thought I have decided boldly to cry "stet!" Let it stand, as long it has stood, including a misspelling of one of the best-known banking institutions of the country. (Wonder if they have fired that proofreader yet?)

What this edition should be is a memoir of how things appeared to me fifteen years ago, after I had been toiling in those perpendicular vineyards for nearly fifteen years before that. A memoir does not require retouching; to do so mars its merits as a memoir. A man like myself chooses the honest way, the easy way!*

The year the book was written was a sluggish one in Wall Street with stocks at low prices—nearly as low as they ever were since the First World War. Since very few people are emotionally stirred by low stock prices, the interest of the public in Wall Street at that time was about the same as its interest, then and now, in court tennis. Only a few traditionally wealthy families take an interest in low stock prices or in court tennis. So the tape moved along like an unbabbling brook, and the brokers had time for backgammon and even book writing.

But in the previous years that I served in that galley with an outboard motor, I had seen just about everything, most of it with wild surprise. First I was

* 1955: The only exception to this will be the addition of a few 1955 footnotes of which this is an example.

privileged to watch the last three years of the so-called "incredible twenties" (and why are they still called incredible?). Then I suddenly had an excellent seat for the Crash, a period of three months, an episode as vivid, tragic, and dramatic as has occurred in our history. Shortly later I was forced to be an unwilling spectator and participant in the Depression. This was far more tragic, and had only the wretched dramatic values of a drab nightmare. It was a dream horrifying and uninteresting at the same time. It seemed to the men of importance, many of them good men, contrary to the popular conception, as impossible to cope with as is any other nightmare before the terrified dreamer can wake up. Then the new President, a man I have generally admired, reopened the banks, using eight of the most effective words ever uttered on the radio (he had previously closed them, with valid reason). The nightmare ended with the blink of an eye, as does any other.

About four years later, in the last half of 1937, there was another little panic but it was neat and orderly. For the next four years nothing much happened in Wall Street, and continued not to happen, day after day, until Pearl Harbor. I speak here, one must understand, strictly of Wall Street. Way out there in the world, plenty had happened.

Shortly after that I left Wall Street, and I believe it was the next day that stocks began going up; they have continued to go up, with all but negligible interruptions, ever since. Probably there is no connection.

I have never gone back to the Street professionally, but I have gone back sometimes as a Customer. The chief difference one might think is that I no longer receive a salary for going down there. But no, the real difference is one of the attitude of the Street to me. Now when I saunter into a brokerage office at half past eleven, no frenetic superior howls at me for being tardy, or stupid, though in my role of customer I have often been both. The cheerful, albeit respectful, courtesy that I invariably receive these days sometimes borders on the fawning, especially if there is something in my bearing that suggests I might be in the mood to trade in fifty shares of something.

If there is anything in the old edition that can be criticized except one misspelling and some immature remarks, it would perhaps be the chapter on investment trusts, as they were then universally called. I seem to have taken a slightly patronizing tone in discussing them. Ever since my mild ironies have appeared in uncancelable type, these corporations have steadily increased in value.

There is infinitely more significance to the rise of these corporations than to any of the more spectacular leaps of some individual stocks during the same period. The vast bulk of them, and now they are vast, are "open-end" investment companies, now named "Mutual Funds."

Mutual Funds are rarely bought at an investor's whim. The management has hard-working and persuasive salesmen out, digging into new territory all over, not just in the stock-conscious coastal areas and big cities. They call on people and explain the advantages of their wares, and answer questions. They call again if they are given any encouragement; they call again if they are not given any encouragement.

They can properly compare to life-insurance sales-men. You remember the life insurance guy: first he was a minor nuisance, then he became loathsome, then he pushed a policy down your throat. Then, a decade or two later, you view your policy fondly, and congratulate yourself on being such a respon-sible citizen and family man.

The way things have gone for fifteen years it can easily be argued that the mutual-funds salesmen have done their reluctant clients an even greater boon than did the life-insurance salesmen. Anyway, so far.

I note at least in my defense that on my page 47 there appeared a footnote that suggested that "in-vestment trust" was an unhappy and inaccurate designation and that something better should be in-vented. This has been done and nobody so far has thanked me. A further small irony is that when I set down my small ironies on the subject, I happened to be the beneficial holder of shares in a good invest-ment trust. These shares, being a "closed-end" com-pany, had not been sold to me by a salesman. I had purchased them, on my own judgment or whim, on the New York Stock Exchange. A few years later, observing that they had all but doubled in value, I judged that this was ridiculous, and sold them, via the New York Stock Exchange, to some faceless stranger, who was a fool for luck. I also did this on my own judgment. My crafty plan was to repurchase them after they had gone down to some more sensible level.

As it happened I never repurchased them because they never went down. Where they have gone up to I don't feel in the mood to discuss just now. For my only comment on my second transaction I must go beyond the confines of the ordinarily rich English Language.

Oy.

Probably no reader has ever been so rude as to inquire of a professional writer on financial matters why the writer, who clearly knows so much about money, is not rich. Nevertheless, many a reader probably thinks quietly about this. Such a reader deserves some attempt at explanation, however inadequate.

In my case I have not only written airily on financial matters but I have actually been fiddling around with common stocks most of my mature life. My passions have rarely been stirred by senior securities. And as of this writing the common-stock market has been going up for fifteen years and is at a new high since ancient Rome. Yet I haven't got a Cadillac to my name.

I lay this mediocre result to the impressionableness of my youth. In those days I used to work at a trading table across from an older man, a cynical Irishman whose cynicism I secretly admired. Oft was I privileged to hear him mutter his favorite bit of logic to himself: "What were securities created for in the first place? They were created to be sold, so sell them."

Ever since, my tendency has been to buy stocks, all a-tremble as I do so. Then when they show a profit I sell them, exultantly. (But never within six months, of course. I'm no anarchist.) It seems to me at these moments that I have achieved life's loveliest guerdon —making some money without doing any work.

Then a long time later it turns out that I should have just bought them, and thereafter I should have just sat on them like a fat, stupid peasant. A peasant, however, who is rich beyond his limited dreams of avarice.

Where Are the Customers' Yachts?

CHAPTER ONE

Introduction

"The Modest Cough of a Minor Poet"

—G. B. S.

"WALL STREET," READS the sinister old gag, "is a street with a river at one end and a graveyard at the other."

This is striking, but incomplete. It omits the kindergarten in the middle, and that's what this book is about.

For a considerable time now the writer has been viewing the activities of this street each working day, usually from the vantage point of a trading table. At such a table we have access to every form of communication except the heliograph. What we are constantly exchanging, over the incredible network of wires, are quotations, orders, bluffs, fibs, lies, and nonsense. The first four are the necessary agenda of doing brokerage in securities. The downright lies are rather exceptional, and in the long run prove to be unprofitable business practice.

The chief concern of this book will be with an examination of the nonsense—a commodity which keeps sluicing in through the weeks and years with the irresistible constancy of the waters of the rolling Mississippi. Wall Street professionals handle the quote-and-fib part of their business with competence, and sometimes with brilliance. Later, when the mood is on them, they add their Thoughts, still under the impression that they are doing an important day's work. We shall also try not to neglect the nonsense contributed freely by customers, legislators, the press, and the public.

I can recall that even on my very first day in Wall Street, early in '27, I heard considerable foolishness. I didn't spot it for that then, or for some time thereafter. This might have been because I had trained for the profession, as had so many others, with an in-

4

tensive course in the liberal arts, with emphasis upon the Romantic poets of the nineteenth century. But I can't honestly testify that the boys who took commercial courses awoke from their dreams one bit sooner than we beauty lovers did.

On that first day of employment I was told to look about and acclimate myself. I observed a gentleman buy two hundred shares of something at eleven o'clock. At half-past two he sold it, and willingly calculated for me his profit, which was five hundred and sixty dollars. Naturally, I stood and watched this operation, quite pop-eyed, with a vague sense of pleasure. After the market had closed, I timidly approached some of the office pundits and asked where that money had come from, and had anybody lost it when the man won it? I received a number of prompt and windy answers, none of which was correct. One gray-thatched Nestor explained to me in a simple and kindly manner that the customer had made this money and that the "shorts" had lost it. A younger man said that that was silly (it was), that no one had lost it, that it was a natural increment accompanying the expansion of American Prosperity (which had apparently expanded at least $560 worth right under my nose in a few hours). A third man confided to me that the customer had made this profit quite easily by merely following an "indelibly indicated trend." A fourth said, emphasizing his pronunciamento by tapping me on the chest with a well-manicured finger, "Young man, a bull makes money, a bear makes money, but a hog never makes anything!"

This last statement, while startling and intriguing, did not seem relevant to my question, even then. It took me some time to discover it to be particularly untrue. I have heard it often since; it is a sort of customers' man's chantey to encourage customers to step into and out of the market a little livelier.

Such expressions as the above are mild and simple samples of financial thinking. They might be called Board-Room Economics. Statistical Department Economics are much more profound or, anyway, more complicated. The reader will not get much of those in this book. The reason is that I wouldn't discuss economic profundities if I could, and besides, I can't.

6

—the customer had made this profit quite easily by merely following an "indelibly indicated trend."

My method of dealing with those subjects which I have never been able to understand will be to omit them, though this is not the customary method of writers on financial topics.

Please realize that if I am asked to define national prosperity, or to give a recipe for attaining it, or to discuss its relation to our present gold holdings, I can begin vaporing as quickly as the next fellow. But it would be twice-breathed vapor, not my own, and for all I have ever been able to make out, mostly vapor when it was new. Although not a Deep Thinker myself, I have had a thousand separate lunches with those who were. Authoritative figures, compiled by the National Association of Laundries, will show conclusively that there is no school of economic thought which hasn't marked up a tablecloth with huge numbers in an effort to show me the way to financial salvation. Sometimes the salvation was for my country; sometimes just for me.

Books about Wall Street fall into two categories which may respectively be called the admiring, or "Oh, my!" School, and the vindictive, or "Turn the

Rascals Out" School. Needless to say, the former were all written formerly, and the latter, latterly, the dividing line being around October, 1929. Neither school assays more than a few pounds of open-mindedness to the ton, and that noble occupation, Deep Thinking, continues to be, as ever, mostly second guessing. This book will try to avoid being classified in either school. The writer has no warm emotional regard for any set of economic theories, and I am not in the pay of either Moscow or The Interests.†

There will be found in this work a scandalous lack of statistical proof. There will be no sentences beginning: "In this connection it is significant to note that reliable figures compiled by a prominent school of business administration reveal that in the first quarter of 1938, $218,350,626.55, or 8¼ per cent of the total income of families of four or more including at least one wage earner, but exclusive of any money derived from dividends or rents, etc., etc., etc."

One can't say that figures lie. But figures, as used

---

† Dammit.

in financial arguments, seem to have the bad habit of expressing a small part of the truth forcibly, and neglecting the other part, as do some people we know. A case in point is that preferred stock you bought as an extra-safe investment several years ago when the salesman showed you that the stock was earning its dividend more than fifty times over. And then one day you found that this preferred stock was not earning its dividend five times, or even one time. It seems that both the figures and the salesman had neglected to point out the unholy size of the funded debt which was senior to your stock.

Of course, in any of these complex matters, if we could be sure we had *all* the figures, plus *all* the pertinent footnotes which to a greater or lesser extent invalidate most of the figures, then we would certainly have something, even if it were only the blind staggers.

On the descriptive side, a plucky effort will be made to describe the people and operations of Wall Street as they really are. We already have the descriptions from the two schools of writers I have mentioned. We have further, in great plenty, descriptions proffered by the presidents of exchanges, by spokesmen for great banks and industries, by New Dealers, Old Dealers, and the S.E.C., by thoughtful radicals writing in ivy-covered towers, and by informal but enthusiastic radicals shouting from soapboxes in Columbus Circle and Union Square. There is nothing surprising in the conclusion that they can't all be right. But it *is* surprising that no one of them is ever quite right. The best explanation is that some of them don't know what they are talking about; and those who do know, don't tell all they know, or don't permit themselves to believe all that they know. To borrow a term from professional wrestling, they don't "level" with us, and this is true of both the Left and the Right.

The Validity of Financial Predictions

On the theoretic side our chief preoccupation will be with an inquiry which is quite simple, but which is more awful in its implications than any Senate investigation. It has to do with what has become the major part of the business of Wall Street—the foretelling of price moves. Concerning these predictions we are about to ask:

1. Are they pretty good?
2. Are they slightly good?
3. Are they any damn good at all?
4. How do they compare with tomorrow's weather prediction you read in the paper?
5. How do they compare with the tipster horse-race services?

The best way for us to pursue our researches in these questions is to hop a subway downtown. (All the subways run to Wall Street: it is a really important place.) We emerge into that famous maze of canyons, the deepest and sheerest in the world. Then through a set of great doors which never cease revolving, and we are whisked upward in a high-speed elevator. In a few moments we are cliff-high above the teeming street, ready to sample our first Financial Prediction.

We find it in a comfortable board room, where the fascinating symbols and figures glide seductively across the translux. It is: "Looks like there will be a little rally after lunch." This is proffered by young Mr. Joseph Wisenheimer, assistant order clerk, who has had two years at Central High. He is leaning against the ticker box, chewing gum, and looking shrewd. He has dropped this little nugget of matured wisdom into a surrounding nest of customers, many of whom are as impressionable as subdebs. At that, the odds against his being correct are hardly worse than two to one against him. When that fateful moment arrives (the conclusion of lunch), it is safe to say that the market will be either higher—or lower—or unchanged.

We now leave these friendly quarters and enter the portals of a suite that smacks more of the cathedral than of commerce. We progress with increasing difficulty past receptionists, beautiful secretaries, and scholarly young acolytes to the gleaming mahogany

We progress with increasing difficulty past receptionists, beautiful secretaries, and scholarly young acolytes to the gleaming mahogany desk of S. Hugo Big.

desk of S. Hugo Big. Here we garner Thought Number Two, which has just been prepared by Mr. Big himself and will immediately go out on all wires. Skipping down to its conclusion:

. . . It therefore becomes clear that over the period of the next fifteen years the investment demand for sound convertible issues bearing a low coupon but carrying an attractive conversion feature will find such deserved popularity with the long-sighted investor as to cause the more classic forms of indenture to look to their laurels.

Now the question is: which of these two statements is the sillier? Either of them, you understand, might be correct. And both of them, or statements much like them, have sold billions of dollars' worth of securities.

Perhaps you veer toward Thought Two because onomatopoeically it has a sillier sound.

This I hardly think is fair. Young Joe doesn't know so many long words. But he claims that he is saying something that has some meaning and he claims it just as definitely as Mr. Big. The latter, having been to the business school at Harvard and also having taken courses in English literature, can make his statement *sound* sillier. But, since neither of them has any factual or causal basis for saying either of these things, I claim the honors are even.

Now it should be said here that neither of these men is a liar or even a faker.

If you ask Joe why there will be a little rally after lunch, he will tell you in no uncertain terms. He will say that he observes that the volume is decreasing on the down side, that he can see that steels are strongly pegged just above the last previous lows, and that "they" (whoever "they" are) † are beginning to accumulate second-grade carriers. "But it won't go very far," he may add, proving that at heart he is no wild-eyed optimist—more the old-line banker type. "'They' wouldn't want to see this market run away."

It is a marvelous thing, the way this lingo is universally used in board rooms, not just in New York but from coast to coast. It is as though someone had

_____

† For an effort to penetrate this mystery, see Chapter VI.

18

invented an Esperanto for saying nothing in a variety of ways.

And, if you ask Mr. Big on what he predicates his fifteen-year opinion, he will give you so many reasons you will wish you had not asked. But he ought to know better. If he should ever lift his nose out of the minutiae of his fascinating business and view it and its history whole, he would be forced to admit the sad truth that pitifully few financial experts have ever known for two years (much less fifteen) what was going to happen to any class of securities—and that the majority are usually spectacularly wrong in a much shorter time than that.

Still he is not a liar; nor is our other friend. I can explain it, because I have not only had lunch with economists, but I have sometimes had dinner with psychiatrists. It seems that the immature mind has a regrettable tendency to believe, as actually true, that which it only hopes to be true. In this case, the notion that the financial future is not predictable is just too unpleasant to be given any room at all in the Wall Streeter's consciousness. But we expect a child to grow up in time and learn what is reality, as opposed to what are only his hopes.

This, however, is asking too much of the romantic Wall Streeter—and they are all romantics, whether they be villains or philanthropists. Else they would never have chosen this business which is a business of dreams. They continue to dream of conquests, coups, and power, for themselves or for the people they advise.

Some Wall Street men manage to shed these dreams, given sufficient years. But the ultimate dream they almost never shed: that there is a secret, meaningful and predictable, in the rise and fall of financial enterprises—that a "close study" of this and that will prove something; that it will tell the initiate when there will be a rally or give the speculator a better than even chance of making a killing, or guarantee for an estate a safe four per cent for a few generations. All these things are demonstrably unpredictable. You can easily check this from your own experience, or by other people's experience, or by looking over the factual matter in the indignation

books. But this cup of tea is too bitter for a Wall
Streeter.

The Passion for Prophecy

The genesis of Wall Street was a buttonwood tree
under which buyers and sellers used to meet. That
tree perfectly fulfilled the pure function of a market
place; it was a known spot where a man could go to
do financial business. A necessary code of procedure
for trading was recognized. But soon the brokers
moved into a near-by coffeehouse and began adding
the business of prophecy to the business of brokerage.
The next thing that happened was that the prophecy
business almost swamped and ruined the brokerage
business.

The croupier at the roulette table does not claim
that he knows something about the order in which
the numbers will come up. He just sees to it that the
bets are properly paid off and that the house isn't
gypped—which is a job requiring competence.

But it is hard to find a Wall Street man, from the oldest partner to the youngest "runner," who is willing to be just a croupier. This causes a great deal of anguish in the long run, and the reasons for it are both human and economic.

For one thing, customers have an unfortunate habit of asking about the financial future. Now if you do someone the signal honor of asking him a difficult question, you may be assured that you will get a detailed answer. Rarely will it be the most difficult of all answers—"I don't know."

The average male likes to sit at breakfast and tell his wife and children what Adolf Hitler is going to do month after next. This is a harmless vanity. But from this it is an easy step for him to go downtown and start telling people what United States Steel is going to do month after next. That is liable to lose someone's life savings for him.

On the economic side there is no denying that the more financial predictions you make the more business you do and the more commissions you get. That, we all know, is not the right way to act at all. But I

The average male likes to sit at breakfast and tell his wife and children what Adolf Hitler is going to do month after next.

doubt if there are many, or any, Wall Streeters who sit down and say to themselves coolly, "Now let's see. What cock-and-bull story shall I invent and tell them today?" I don't think you can supply any guarantee of accuracy when looking into the heart and mind of someone else. But I feel, from years of personal observation, that the usual thought process is far more innocent. The broker influences the customer with his knowledge of the future, but only after he has convinced himself. The worst that should be said of him is that he wants to convince himself badly and that he therefore succeeds in convincing himself—generally badly.

The runners (the young fellows—sometimes old fellows—who hustle through the financial district delivering securities and calling for checks) have at least as many opinions about future prices as the oldest partner, although they have nothing whatever to gain by having them. You can hear them in the elevators, acting as unpaid investment counsel to the elevator operators. But the best proof of the predictors' confused sincerity is that they are constantly sampling their own medicine. At the present time the Securities and Exchange Commission is still formulating new rules in an attempt to limit this convincing form of hara-kiri.

When a great and sagacious financier dies, and the executors go through the strongbox, they usually find, tucked well away in the back, bundles of the most hopeless securities whose very names have been long since forgotten. Although these executors will never leave an estate worth a tenth as much as this one, they gaze at the bundles with wonder and amusement. "Golly," they say, "whatever could the old man have been thinking of to get stuck with these cats and dogs?"

When the Bull Jumped Over the Moon

It may have been observed that while arguing my case against the validity of financial predictions, I have not touched on the most spectacular example— the late twenties, the supreme miscalculation of this

century, which Mr. Westbrook Pegler always refers
to as "the era of wonderful nonsense." I have avoided
this for several reasons. For one thing, it is too easy
and has been cited too many thousand times by people who, ten years ago, were, like everyone else, its
dupes. For another thing it was not in all respects
Wall Street's error. It was one of the great universal
delusions of history, somewhat comparable to such
magnificent errors as that the world was flat, or that
all you had to do to heal anybody of anything was to
bleed him.

There is a feeling in some quarters that even in the
late twenties there were crafty Wall Streeters who
knew the market was too high. Sure there were, but
it didn't do many of them much good. Mr. Andrew
Mellon was heard to murmur something to the effect
that "gentlemen prefer bonds," but it was not established whether this was his considered advice or a
belated entry into wittiness. Mr. Roger Babson had
predicted the crash for several years, which shows,
among other things, that he had been very wrong for
several years before he suddenly became very right.

27

There was always a scattering of bears, "aginners" by temperament, who spent their business days having their ears knocked off. Many of them, bowing to a force which finally seemed cosmic, switched to being bulls at a sadly late period in the era. The remainder who were still short at the time of the crash covered too soon (as who wouldn't?). Then, after prices had gone inconceivably lower, they took their profits and bought stocks (as who wouldn't?). In due course of time, if they bought on margin, they went to "the Cleaners," that mythical establishment to which their brother speculators had repaired some time earlier. "The Cleaners" was not one of those exclusive clubs; by 1932 everybody who had ever tried speculation had been admitted to membership.

CHAPTER TWO

Financiers and Seers

T O CATALOGUE ALL the different jobs in Wall Street would be lengthy rather than interesting. The subdivisions of functions are endless. For instance, the technique of trading government bonds over telephones is distinctly different from trading real-estate bonds over telephones. (In 1929 I knew a boy who received $25 a week for untangling telephone cords on a large trading desk. If that wasn't prosperity, what was?)

Let's consider some of the broader classifications. We might as well start at the top and work down— a not unusual Wall Street method of pursuing a career. First there is the cream of the crop—the truly conservative banker.

Big Banking—Nice Work If You Can Get It

The conservative banker is an impressive specimen, diffusing the healthy glow which comes of moderation in eating, living, and thinking. He sits in state and spends his days saying, with varying inflections and varying contexts, "no." He is at the top, or close to the top, of one of those financial empires whose destinies have been guided with such prudence, shrewdness, and soundness that today the Great House has darn near as much money and prestige as it had in 1900.

He says "yes" only a few times a year. His rule is that he reserves his yesses for organizations so wealthy that if he said "no," some other banker would quickly say "yes." His business might be defined as the lending of money exclusively to people who have no pressing need of it. In times of stress, when everybody needs money, he strives to avoid lending to anybody, but usually makes an exception of the United States government.

Likewise, in prosperous times he is a mighty liberal

lender—so liberal that years later unfriendly committees ask him what he thought he was thinking about, and he is unable to remember clearly.

With all this, I believe he does the best job of the lot. Years have gone by, and he hasn't been indicted —there haven't even been any bad scandals; some of the accounts haven't lost anything, and the others have at least lost their money gradually, not suddenly. When the great man is asked for investment advice, he immediately picks out something triple-A. The income from this will be at a very small rate, but that won't matter, only provided the investor is as rich as the banker. Investments of this type have only a very small chance of going down in value, and no chance of going up. If the cost of living should rise, the investor may find that he is having difficulty with his rent and groceries, but he will have nothing specific with which to reproach the banker. His bonds will still be quoted at a figure not shockingly below what he paid for them.

Your truly conservative banker cannot be stampeded into unwary speculations by the hysteria of a boom. He reminds me a little of what I once heard one doctor say of another: "He doesn't know enough medicine to do a patient any harm." He sits tight through '26, '27, and '28. Unfortunately, he begins to come into the market in '29. He begins cautiously enough, like an old maid trying out lipstick in the privacy of her room. (Watching these young whippersnappers make fortunes for three long years does something to the sturdiest character.) But he pulls out again, and, while a nice piece of money is lost, no one is ruined. He apologizes to himself for having had a human moment and resumes his thirty-year-old policy of listening attentively and saying "no."

Way back, generations ago, when it was smart to be tough, the original hundred millions were gathered together in some more realistic business—say, selling firewater to the Indians. And these present grandsons of fortune, sitting up there in a courteous trance, are perhaps not so dumb as they look. I just suspect that they too consider that buying and selling securities is a poor occupation—at least for the customer. But they don't publish tracts explaining this to the public; they just personally avoid it as much as they can without losing the franchise.

After these great and established bankers come all sorts of lesser bankers. The lesser bankers are under the unfortunate necessity of saying "yes" more frequently. This is because the ideal borrowers (people who don't need the money) do not come to them. *Their* clients need the money, and the lesser bankers must occasionally get it for them, or else close up shop and, God forbid! go home and relax. Like most other Wall Streeters, bankers suffer from the inability to do nothing. Your average Wall Streeter, faced with nothing profitable to do, does nothing for only a brief time. Then, suddenly and hysterically, he does something which turns out to be extremely unprofitable. He is not a lazy man.

Prosperous brokers labor under a constant urge to become nonprosperous bankers. The reasons for this are obscure; probably it is a sort of social climbing. But it is a sad sight. Here we have a broker who for years has been collecting bushel baskets of nice little commissions. Suddenly we find him blossoming forth

33

as a minor banker. He is gathering together half a million dollars (largely from himself and his mother-in-law). With these funds he will promote the manufacture and sale of a new fuel for automobiles which is cheaper than gasoline, odorless, and noninflammable, but which, it later turns out, will not make an automobile run, except on very warm, windless days.

Some Assistant Tycoons

The public has very little chance to enjoy personal contact with great bankers because of the unfortunate fact that so few of the public are rich. It is easier for a poor man to go through the eye of a needle than it is for him to get past a rich man's receptionists. We shall now take up some categories of financial men who are easier to see. Such are partners, customers' men,† heads of trading departments, and statisticians.

---

† A new name is being sought for "customers' man." As this is being written, "registered representative" is being considered, but I do not think it will be retained simply because "registered representative" is too much of a mouthful.

Even here the tendency is for important partners to be accessible only to the larger accounts, and so on down the scale to the least successful customers' man, who is only too anxious to talk to anybody about anything. A customers' man whose phone rarely rings does not look well sitting at a desk gazing into space. He should take up some outside interest, like college football, and discuss this topic in a low voice over the phone with his friends. It tends to spruce up his appearance, and the office's, too.

All these gentlemen have needful functions in which they should be engaged. Unfortunately, such is their zeal that they not only perform their functions but throw in a line of prophecy for good measure. Statisticians should be gathering statistics, and wire traders should be busy with the fine art of wire trading. Partners have many difficult administrative problems besides acting as customers' men for their own clients. The proper activity of a customers' man is to keep his clients informed as to what is happening and what has happened. To these services he insists on adding, as I have complained already, his notions of what is going to happen. So do nearly all the others, and the property damage that results compares favorably, or dismally, with that caused by the Japanese beetle.

Partners have private offices, sometimes paneled in attractive hardwoods, in which to have their Thoughts, while the customers' men have to spawn theirs in public out in the board room. The type of customer who habitually sits in a board room is frequently just a gent who loves to chat in masculine company but who doesn't belong to a club. This makes the board room a difficult place for profound thinking. Nevertheless, the customers' men manage to reach the same unfortunate conclusions as the partners.

I hold in sincere admiration those men who successfully "make markets" and trade "on the wires," i.e., by telephones, teletype, and telegram. It is a technical sort of game requiring a number of special talents, including memory, mathematics, reputation, and the ability both to make bluffs and to see through them. The more skillful of these traders can, and do,

The type of customer who habitually sits in a board room is frequently just a gent who loves to chat in masculine company but who doesn't belong to a club.

peer into the future for a period of five or even twenty minutes concerning those securities which they are actively trading. This short-term peering is a legitimate function because plenty of hints are pouring in to them all the time on many wires. However, as soon as they get a moment of leisure they try peering into the future for five or ten months. For this they are precisely as ill equipped as everybody else.

The statisticians are housed way down the hall in scholarly quiet. No noisy tickers or loquacious customers are allowed to intrude, and the Thinkers are surrounded by tomes of reference and the latest news flashes from everywhere. They all carry slide rules, which as everyone knows are more scientific than divining rods. They make exhaustive studies of many a "special situation" and eventually get to know absolutely everything about the affairs of a certain corporation, except perhaps one detail, which is that shortly after the inception of the ensuing fiscal year, the corporation is going into 77B.†

---

† A gentler form of bankruptcy invented by the New Deal, but still bankruptcy; now called Chap. 10 of the Chandler Act.

When a statistician works up a sufficient reputation for profundity, he is graduated and becomes an economist. There was one economist who never went anywhere without his many brief cases, which were the fattest and heaviest known to the fiscal world. He was in big demand and attended conferences all over, but he was not an athletic type, so office boys had to lug the brief cases. I once found myself in an elevator with one of these boys. He was sagging under the brief cases and looked like a melancholy dray horse.

"Those belong to Mr. Z?" I asked.

"Uh-huh," he replied, with no enthusiasm.

"Listen," I said. "Here is an idea. Why don't you kids paste a little strip of paper inside the zippers? Then you could find out whether he ever opens those brief cases."

"We did," said the moody office boy. "He don't."

Some statisticians have to write weekly, and even daily, "market letters." This is a tough way to make a living. It not only requires the constant making of predictions, but it requires putting the predictions down on paper for anyone interested to check up on. Sometimes these letters come back with a jug of mustard and a forcible suggestion that the writer apply the mustard to his letter and eat it. Statisticians of a nervous, sensitive sort, after a few such experiences, develop a prose style which would make a German nineteenth-century metaphysician envious. Here is a favorite I clipped out of *The Wall Street Journal* once and have carried around proudly until it is now almost as illegible as it is incomprehensible. The *Journal* printed it under the questionable heading, "Market Ideas—"

A leading brokerage house says: "During the slow rise from the April lows which carried the Dow-Jones industrial average from approximately 121 to the 139 level, the action of the market was regarded as in the nature of a technical recovery, with little thought of the imminence of dynamic action. Resistance, as expected, was encountered just under 140; but after a one-day decline, volume dwindled, and the market presently appears to be engaged in a somewhat hazy consolidation movement, and perhaps searching for dynamic forces which will encourage broad gauge buying and the resulting demolition of resistance barriers."

If the thoughtful reader will now read that statement backwards he will discover that its original lucidity is not impaired. I have composed a guitar accompaniment to go with it, beginning with that mystic section, "—and the market presently appears—" The piece is surprisingly effective, and will be used as the underlying motif in a forthcoming surrealist ballet.

The Fruit on the Blossom of Thought

When they do express opinions, the statisticians and economists manage to come to the same general conclusions as do the partners and the customers' men. If these conclusions can be generalized, the underlying principle may be loosely stated thus: buy them when they are up, and sell them when the margin clerk insists on it.

It is obviously impossible for the thinking Wall

42

Streeter to avoid acting on that principle. He certainly can't buy them when they are down, because when they are down "conditions" are terrible. You can't ask an experienced Wall Street man to buy stocks when carloadings have just hit a new low and unemployment is at a peak and steel capacity is less than half of normal and a very big man ("of course I can't tell you his name") has just informed him in confidence that one of the big underwriting houses in the Middle West is in really serious trouble.

Unfortunately for everyone concerned, these are the only times when stocks are down. When "conditions" are good, the forward-looking investor buys. But when "conditions" are good, stocks are high. Then, without anyone having the courtesy to ring a warning bell, "conditions" get bad. Stocks go down, and the margin clerk sends the forward-looking investor a telegram containing the only piece of financial advice he will ever get from Wall Street which has no ifs or buts in it.

43

Wall Street Semantics

There are a couple of common phrases which do their share in perpetuating this ancient vicious practice of buying them when they are high and selling them when they are low. These two phrases are the usual reply to the inquiry, "What is the market doing?" The answering phrases are—"It is going up," or, "It is going down." I wish that instead of finding a new name for "customers' man" someone would find a proper predicate to take the place of these two. The nearest I can suggest is, "Up to this moment, transactions have been occurring at continuously higher prices." But that is too wordy.

It is a fair thing to say of a piston, an elevator, or a golf ball at a certain moment, that it is "going up." This suggests not only that it has been going up, but that it will probably continue to go on up, for a little time at least, because whatever impulse started it is still operating to some extent. But it is not a fair thing to say of the stock market, which, not being a physical thing, is not subject to Newton's laws of propulsion

44

or inertia. Unfortunately most of us unconsciously credit this false analogy. Thus we are not tempted to buy unless they are "going up" or to sell unless they are "going down." But when the market is "going up" like fury, there is no reason to believe that the very next "tick" is more likely to be up than down. But that, children, is how Grandfather got himself whipsawed, as the faro players say.

Chartists

I have purposely left for separate consideration the Chart Readers, a small, passionate sect. Their business definitely is to predict the future and if they are unable to do this they will have to find some other employment. Long-term forecasting is their *raison d'être*.

This writer does not believe that they can predict the future with any useful accuracy, nor can he perceive what there is in their methods which should persuade anyone to think that they can. Some people, however, believe in the charts implicitly, and many more take a peculiar half-and-half position. Major Angas,† for instance, after describing several American chart systems, concludes, in a fine burst of inconclusiveness: "All of these theories are true part of the time; none of them all the time. They are, therefore, dangerous, though sometimes useful." The same could be said of the practice of flipping a coin to determine whether one should buy or sell—all except the word "useful," which doesn't seem to be admissible in either case. Chart theories are indeed "useful" in bringing in a certain type of customer, but Major Angas is not referring to that.

Your properly consecrated chart reader pays no attention to "conditions" at all—neither flood, famine, pestilence, nor war. He arms himself with a chart (the simplest sort of graph) which depicts the ups and downs in price of the market as a whole or of a

---

† Major L. L. B. Angas is one of the most outspoken and dramatic of public forecasters and has made a number of impressive predictions. So far as I know, he uses charts sparingly if at all. The quotation is from his book, *Investment for Appreciation.*

46

commodity. This he studies, well away from the news ticker. It is his claim that he can discern in this jagged line a pattern of behavior which reproduces itself and that certain of the peaks, valleys, and wobbles tell him when it is about to do it again. His technical jargon contains such phrases as "head-and-shoulders formation," "double tops," "double bottoms," and "breakaway gaps."

This is the baldest description of charts. The subject can be spun out into extravagant complexity and it frequently is. It is only necessary to plot into the graph carloadings, bank clearances, government bond yields, and sunspots.

There have always been a considerable number of pathetic people who busy themselves examining the last thousand numbers which have appeared on a roulette wheel, in search of some repeating pattern. Sadly enough, they have usually found it.

It would serve no purpose, nor would it be fair, for me, an unsympathetic citizen, to try to explain the technical secrets of chart reading. I have had the subject explained to me a number of times, but perhaps I have missed some central point which would give the whole theory credence. I am far from being alone in this; smarter men than I have often been unable, or unwilling, to pursue this science far. As a science, I should say that chart reading shares a pedestal with astrology; but most chart readers are educated men and have too much mental discipline to take astrology seriously.

The subject seems to suffer from a lack of causation. When the student peers, however closely, at a graph of the Dow-Jones averages, for instance, all he sees for certain is a history of past performances clearly and conveniently depicted. That one can, by examining the line already drawn, make a useful guess at the line not yet drawn, must be predicated on the hypothesis that "history repeats itself." History does in a vague way repeat itself, but it does it slowly and ponderously, and with an infinite number of surprising variations. But the chartists are trying to use the analogy to predict, with some precision, prices from month to month and for even shorter periods. It is a little reminiscent of those farmer's almanacs

48

which without apology calmly predict the weather for the next 365 days. While the editors of these almanacs have perceived, by examining past performances, that it gets hot each summer and cold each winter, they do not do at all well in calling their shots day by day.

I once suggested to a chart reader, who was explaining his theories to me, that since I wasn't a customer he should slip me the wink on this tripe. It was a social error: he was as deeply offended as if I had said something gross about his religion—which, I suppose, I had.

All I was ever able to conclude from my informal studies was that chart reading is a complex way of arriving at a simple theorem, to wit: when they have gone up for a considerable time, they will continue to go up for a considerable time; and the same holds true for going down.

This is simple, but it does not happen to be so. The easiest way of perceiving that it is not so is to go get a properly drawn chart and look at it.

It is the popular feeling in Wall Street that chart

49

readers are pretty occult professors but that somehow most of them are broke. A busted chart reader, however, is never apologetic about his method—he is, if anything, more enthusiastic than the solvent devotee you may run across. If you have the bad taste to ask him how it happens that he is broke, he tells you quite ingenuously that he made the all too human error of not believing his own charts. This naïve thought comforts him; he doesn't mind so much losing his money, but it would have been more than he could stand to lose his faith in his beloved chart system.

The Pay

It is now high time that we took up a matter of universal curiosity whenever any sort of commercial work is under discussion—how much do they pay those fellows? Since this subject is nobody's business, everyone is interested. As the man said after he had had the subject of relativity explained to him in a few unsuccinct phrases: "And from this Mr. Einstein makes a living?"

Since I do not know how much money Wall Street men make, and since I can think of no reliable way of finding out, I shall promptly answer as follows:

Wall Street, including such suburbs as South La Salle Street, Montgomery Street, Market Street, State Street, Walnut Street, etc., is a community where more than 10,000 different people make more than ten thousand dollars a year. That's more than one hundred million dollars, which, as the boys put it, is not hay.

The above statement, like poetry, is merely used to suggest an idea. The idea is the debatable one that Wall Street is the highest paying spot on the face of the earth. The statement also resembles poetry in that all its details are grossly inaccurate. The above figures have been gathered, without much trouble, out of the top of the writer's head.

Wrong as these figures may be at the moment, they still vary exceedingly in different years. A decade ago one could have said with more confidence that 25,000 people made more than twenty-five thousand dollars a year. And at other periods since then it would have read that only a very few people managed to make even a very few dollars.

It is not only the figures that are vague. The use of the verb "make" is impure. In common usage, "to make $10,000 a year" suggests that the money is earned in salaries and/or commissions. But the bulk of that hundred million is not "earned"—it is won. And then let us not forget that frequently it is not won, it is lost.

Taking all these factors into consideration, we may state with confidence that Wall Street *is* the highest paying spot on the face of the earth, except that maybe it isn't.

The Difficulties of "Earning" Money

There is a small percentage of talented souls who actually "earn" more than ten thousand. Such, for instance, are those few men with such a reputation for sagacity that they are paid a straight salary, and a large one, for advice. There are some partners and customers' men with a large and faithful following of customers who can be truly said to earn their generous incomes from commissions (provided they stay away from that near-by order window themselves).

But now let us take the case of another man who certainly seems to earn his keep. He is what is known as a "two-dollar broker" on the floor of the New York Stock Exchange. His is a "clean" business, without any dubious or expensive odds and ends. He derives his income entirely from small commissions he receives from other brokers for executing orders for them. His office is only desk room, his staff is a clerk or two, his overhead is negligible. All his banking requirements are supplied to him for a very reasonable fee by a larger house, which "clears" for him. He avoids speculation for himself as he would narcotics. Since he never deals with the public, he never has anything on his conscience no matter where the market goes.

Since he is efficient, dependable, and popular, he gets plenty of business. The result is that over the past ten years he has averaged yearly net earnings of

$20,000. *But,* some ten years ago he paid $300,000 for his seat. (Not long after it was worth double that.) Now it is worth less than $100,000. After ten years of faithful and successful work, we must now inquire:

(1) How much has he made?
(2) How would it have been if he had just stayed at home with his $300,000?

The above case has been cited for its stark simplicity, but neither in Wall Street nor corporate enterprise are there any accounting problems quite so simple as that. Bookkeepers and order clerks can find out what they are earning by subtracting their lunches from their salaries, but above that point all accounting problems grow increasingly chaotic.

A large firm has many partners, many seats, great earning capacity, great capital outlay, amazing overhead, and all sorts of securities. Each evening the workers in the "cage" are not allowed to go home until the books "balance." But it is frequently most diffi-

How would it have been if he had just stayed at home with his $300,000?

cult to ascertain whether the firm is making or losing money.

I know of a banking institution whose local rule is that the bookkeepers may not go home if there is a "difference" of more than six cents. Nevertheless it is quite impossible for anyone to state, at any time, what they are really worth within a couple of million dollars.

An Art Without a Muse

Accounting, some say, is not a science but an art. One who held this view, but inarticulately, was an aged gentleman who owned a sizable department store in a Middle Western city. I offer his private method of accounting, for what it is worth, to any puzzled Wall Street partner or proprietor.

The old gentleman was being annoyed by his sons and his auditors, who were trying to show him that while business seemed to be good, the store was actually losing money. They were awash in ledgers and statements, as they strove to prove their point. Finally the old man spoke to them.

"Listen," he said. "The pushcart that I pushed into this town forty years ago we still have. It is in the storeroom on the sixth floor. Go up and look at it. Check it off. Then everything else you see is profit."

Since 1938 a not implausible argument could be presented to show that accounting is not even an art, but just a state of mind. In that year occurred those two fantastic accounting cases—McKesson and Robbins, and Interstate Hosiery Mills. For some time both corporations had flourished like the green bay tree, chiefly on assets that simply weren't there, but which everyone thought were there. Everyone, that is, save one man in each case, who had created the assets all by himself, using only a pen, some ink, and a lot of skillful dishonesty. Presumably these corporations' securities would never have taken those two dives if only the nonexistent assets had not been destroyed by having their nonexistence discovered.

At this point, the subject should be taken away from the accountants and handed over to the metaphysicians. Bishop Berkeley propounded the classic question: if a great tree falls in the forest, does it

58

make any noise if no one is there to hear it fall? He decided it doesn't, which for all I know is the right answer. If the Bishop were living today, I believe he would be interested in this question: if a great corporation is toppling over, does it do anyone any financial harm if no one knows that it is toppling over?

A Little Aptitude Test

As an appendix to this chapter I should like to give some hints as to which young men should, and which should not, take up finance as a career. Wall Street has always been burdened by having in its personnel a good many otherwise estimable people who don't know anything about the laws of probability and risk, and not too much about arithmetic. It should not be too radical to suggest that a young man entering the Street should have some special mental equipment beyond one complete set of smoking-room stories about Mr. and Mrs. Roosevelt.

Of course, if you have a persuasive and forceful

character you can always make a big splash in the Street. You can sell huge amounts of securities, and put over big deals, and combine great corporations. Even if you should botch these matters to a fare-thee-well, you will still be in demand. However, if you can wheedle, charm, cajole, or shout down others, you can make a whacking success anywhere else in commerce. So if you do not happen to be good at judging risks realistically, it would be kinder to exercise that talent in other fields. Try selling cantilever bridges or organizing the revolution.

Test yourself on these six questions. If you have to hesitate in answering them, count the answer wrong.

(1) Do you perceive quite clearly what is the objection to playing a roulette wheel that has two zeros on it? (If not, don't bother to be a financier; be a roulette player.)

(2) If a man has tossed a coin "heads" four times in succession, which do you think he is more likely to toss the fifth time, heads or tails? (If you think he is more likely to toss either heads or tails, look into the interior-decorating game. You have that instinctive

type of mentality which might do very well at that.)

(3) When do you consider that it is a good purchase to draw one card to an inside straight? (Answer
—when you are playing for soybeans.)

(4) If you have answered (3) correctly, do you
find that when you are actually playing poker for
money, you can always resist making that draw? (If
not, stay home with your money and start practicing
being a miser.)

(5) If a stock which is not paying any dividend
is split two for one, how much good does that do the
stockholder? (If you think it does him any real good,
come down and join our sales department, but steer
clear of our trading department.)

(6) What is the primary purpose of a business enterprise? This question is specifically for young men
considering entering the banking field, where they
will have a constant parade of business propositions
passing before them, and they will be required to
plump for a few of them and say "no" to the others.
The answer is elementary and obvious: the primary
purpose of a business is to make money. Almost any-

one knows this with the top part of his brain. But there are only a few valuable young men who also know this all up and down their spinal column.

Most businessmen imagine that they are in business to make money, and that this is their chief reason for being in business, but more often than not they are gently kidding themselves. There are so many other things which are actually more attractive. Some of them are: to make a fine product or to render a remarkable service, to give employment, to revolutionize an industry, to make oneself famous, or at least to supply oneself with material for conversation in the evening. I have observed businessmen whose chief preoccupation was to try to prove conclusively to their competitors that they themselves were smart and that their competitors were damn fools—an effort which gives a certain amount of mental satisfaction but no money at all. I have even seen some whose chief interest lay in proving this point to their partners.

So give yourself a real good mark if you know that a business should make money, but only if you really know it.

62

CHAPTER THREE

Customers—That Hardy Breed

A CUSTOMER MAY BE
loosely defined as anyone who is willing to put up
some money. Lack of customers is the terrible occupational disease of brokers. First the commissions fall
off while the overhead marches on. The next thing
that almost always happens is even worse. The brokers have nothing much to do all day and eventually
even backgammon gets tiresome. So they begin to
play the market themselves, using their own money
instead of the customers'. It is like a saloonkeeper
taking to drink in a slack season, and the results are
about the same. I have known partners, upon forming
a firm, to swear terrible oaths to each other that they

will never operate for their own account. But the urge to become a customer is strong in everybody, even brokers. If they are stockbrokers, they may be able to resist the temptation to trade in stocks, but let someone come in with a fascinating speculation in November hides, or Chinese tael, and they are off. I once heard a Stock Exchange member complain bitterly about his partner. He said, "We would be doing all right except for one thing. Every time I go out to lunch, some curb broker sneaks in here and sells Henry something!"

Varieties of Customers

There are many sorts of customers besides hopeful individuals. Savings banks and life-insurance companies are customers; and they are the very best ones to have if you can get them. Not only is their volume of business large, but you never have to send them margin calls, because that nasty old government does not allow them to exercise their full genius as investors. Then there are many other types of corporations which are splendid customers to have, especially investment trusts and fire-insurance companies.

Other satisfactory types of customers are large estates, or even a brace of wealthy aunts. A rich family finds it an attractive investment to get one or two of its younger males jobs on the strength of handling the family funds. If the firm will pay the young fellow $150 a week, that is just like investing a quarter of a million for him. However, it would be best if the young man in question be of a somewhat cynical cast of mind and more on the lazy than the ambitious side. Otherwise he is liable to try his hand at doubling the estate, and that might be the end of the estate. A good job is worth much fine gold, but it is not worth all the gold.

The great majority of customers are individuals, ranging from rich people and prosperous businessmen (who, presumably, know what they are doing) on down the scale. At the bottom we find a large number of tiny accounts, alternately hopeful and desperate. These people, with next to nothing in the

65

bank and no life insurance, have fallen into the pernicious habit of owning a thousand dollars' worth of common stock against which they owe a debit balance of four hundred and some odd dollars, plus interest.

This last condition was far more prevalent a few years ago before the authorities took steps to curtail margin buying for small accounts. I have often heard it argued that this is a free country and that if a rich man may take a flier, why not a poor man? That is a good argument but I still don't agree with it and will therefore refuse to discuss it further.

How to Get Customers

The simplest way of getting wealthy customers, as I have indicated, is to be born unto them. Failing that, a personable young Wall Streeter can often marry them—I have known cases where it was only necessary to woo them. Some of these customers after a long period of wooing lose their attractiveness both as customers and as brides.

66

Otherwise customers are obtained by much the same mysterious methods whereby doctors get patients and lawyers clients. This is done by circulating around and impressing people with one's talents. This can be done, for instance, by playing an expert game of bridge, because this shows what a head you have on you for figuring out complex matters and winding up with more money. Oddly enough, it can be done even better by playing an expert game of golf, though this only proves that you have a strong and supple back.

Nongame players have to content themselves with looking as wise as steel-rimmed pince-nez and the natural expressions of their faces permit. All candidates stud their conversation with interesting and exciting anecdotes about how their firm sold everything out two weeks ago just before the big decline started. They had stocked up at the beginning of the year just before the sustained rise. It seems they got a confidential report from Washington. (I believe they refer to Washington, D. C., not George Washington.)

The reason traffic moves so slowly on lower Broadway is because it is impeded by swarms of customers' men who have never been wrong once in the last ten years, in retrospect.

In 1928 I knew a customers' man named Tommy who had his own method of getting new customers. It wasn't a very good way, but it was his way. It consisted of having the desk nearest the door. Whenever a stranger came through the door, Tommy would beat the office boy to him and would ask if he could be of service. It seemed like trying to catch trout with a bent pin, but in 1928 Tommy could do it. For instance, one day there appeared a youth who bore in his hand a strange device. Tommy was on him like a flash.

"Can I do anything for you?" he asked politely.

"Well," said the youth, "I would like to see the man that I should talk to about putting a thing on the telephone so nobody can hear what you are saying except you and it is also more sanitary."

"I beg pardon?"

"I would like to see the man that I should——"

68

"I'm sorry, but that man just went out to lunch," said Tommy. "But won't you sit down?"

The youth gratefully sat down and Tommy sold him 200 Anaconda rights. It was the beginning of a short and unprofitable association.

Margin

Americans find margin trading a particularly attractive little invention. It parallels the American principle that the first thing a man should do with his home, even before moving in, is to put it in hock. The idea is that he only has to pay six per cent or so on the mortgage and if he can't wangle something better than a measly six per cent out of a round lot of money, he ought not to be in business. This is another argument I am unable and unwilling to discuss further.

The idea is easily extended to margin trading. We assume that it is a wise and profitable venture to buy 100 shares of United Fido at ten, paying $1,000 for it. Ergo, wouldn't it be even better to buy 200 shares

69

paying the same $1,000? And even better to make it three or four hundred if we can find a sufficiently kindly broker to do us this favor?

The answer is no. But I only know one way of proving it to you conclusively. Go try it.

In trying it, you must use real money. Making "mind bets" won't do. Like all of life's rich emotional experiences, the full flavor of losing important money cannot be conveyed by literature. Art cannot convey to an inexperienced girl what it is truly like to be a wife and mother. There are certain things that cannot be adequately explained to a virgin either by words or pictures. Nor can any description that I might offer here even approximate what it feels like to lose a real chunk of money that you used to own.

Margin requirements are now universally fixed, but formerly many customers used to shop around in different houses to see where they could buy the most stock for the least pledge of money. When they finally found the ultimate "bargain" it frequently entitled them to the privilege of beginning suffering almost immediately instead of waiting awhile for

There are certain things that cannot be adequately explained to a virgin either by words or pictures.

the thumbscrew. As Mr. Eddie Cantor phrased it years ago—"They told me to buy this stock for my old age. It worked wonderfully. Within a week I was an old man!"

Some of the customers who went seeking slim margin requirements actually intended to act conservatively. That is, they only intended to make a quick turn for a modest profit. Also, they expected to limit themselves to a small loss, but this was more vague in their minds. It is easy to take a small profit, but taking a small loss is frequently just a good intention. Eventually the customer finds himself throwing good money after bad, until there isn't any good money left.

I have heard an old-line broker describe this common occurrence. He explained,

"They got on the Twentieth Century Limited at Grand Central Station. They only intended to ride as far as 125th Street, where they would get off and visit Grandma. But the first thing they knew they were making seventy miles an hour through Fort Wayne, Indiana."

What to Do When the Dam Bursts

If you are a customer receiving margin calls there are a number of things you can do, but none of them is good. Probably the best thing to do is to use the Natural-Instinctive method. This consists of picking up a telephone and telling the broker to go climb up a rope, or do anything else with a rope that his fancy dictates, but you won't send him any more money. This has some definite advantages, not the least of them being that it helps relieve the feelings. The broker will sell you out and will then mail you some odd change that is left over. Since this amount is too small to put back in the bank, you will probably do something really useful with it like putting linoleum on the kitchen floor. If the stocks that were sold out immediately start booming upwards again you can meet that difficulty by ceasing to read the financial page.

The second method is to get hold of some more money (Lord knows how but you always can), and send it in. This is known as the Finger-in-the-Dike

—*telling the broker to go climb up a rope, or do anything else with a rope that his fancy dictates.*

method. It is a curious and terrible thing, but for some reason it is easier for a man to raise a thousand dollars for a margin call than it is for him to raise the price of supper if he is starving. This method often works, but it is also the method used by suicides.

The third method is surprisingly popular. This is the Head-in-the-Sand method and is used by those many customers who have in them a strong dash of ostrich. As soon as they read in the paper that their stocks are down, they arrange not to hear about it officially. They refuse to answer telephones or accept telegrams, and in some cases actually make for the Maine woods. Just what they hope to gain by this procedure is problematic. What always happens is that the brokers sell them out as they do with those using method number one. However, the sell-out may come a little later, which means that instead of some small change remaining for the customer, the customer owes the broker the small change.

Sometimes, long afterwards, the ostrich type of customer sues the broker in court, claiming that he never received proper notice of the margin call. If at that time the customer was deeply enough hidden in the Maine woods he probably didn't get proper notice, at that. The customer can do all right in the lower courts, before a jury, because the only thing the average jury comprehends entirely in these cases is that they don't like brokers. But if any real amount of money is involved, the broker appeals the verdict, and a higher court, without a jury, tosses the customer out.

I once knew a professor of English literature who used to receive margin-call telegrams which were sent collect. Not only would he put up the required margin but he would pay for the telegrams as well. While I have in general no useful advice on what to do about margin calls, I definitely feel that you ought not to pay telegram charges on them.

Some Case Histories and a Diagnosis

There will always be customers of a certain mentality who cannot rid themselves of the idea that the whole business is a contest between broker and customer to see which one gets the other's money. Some of them still believe in their hearts that the money they lost in 1929 became the property of their brokers. They secretly continue to believe this after lengthy explanations. The notion that all those greenbacks just evaporated seems to them fanciful.

I am still moved when I recall a gallant little customer in 1928. The market was having a sinking spell, rare for that year, and this man received a margin call for seven hundred dollars. This meant that the house would be pleased to get seven hundred dollars because that would save wear and tear later on, but that in a pinch they could use four hundred, at least until the market went lower. The customer said in high excitement, "Okay, okay, don't close me out, I'll get it!" In quick time a Western Union messenger arrived with five hundred dollars and a note that the rest would soon be forthcoming. At noon another hundred dollars appeared and at half-past one a pathetic twenty-five. At three o'clock, when he had been quite forgotten, he called up.

"You got me," he said with the quiet desperation of Billy the Kid with his last cartridge gone. "I can't raise the last seventy-five. I give up."

Then again, there was the customer who was wise, and fabulously rich. His richness, early in 1929, consisted of seven and a half million dollars,† mostly gained in the past three years. His wisdom lay in this: he put a million and a half dollars into Liberty bonds and gave them to his wife with a forceful presentation speech. "My dearest," he said, "these securities are now yours; they are not mine. They represent quite as much income as we shall ever really need for the rest of our lives. I shall continue to speculate and make more money. But if by any incredible chance I should ever come to you and ask for these bonds back again, under no circumstances give them to me, for you will then know that I have gone crazy."

Six months later he needed margin, further to protect the six million which, he was certain, was only

---

† A large and foolish amount of money, but far short of the record.

temporarily gone. He went for the money to the wife of his bosom, who demurred. But he was a persuasive man: he got the bonds back. Temporarily.

All of the foregoing customers were afflicted with that common psychiatric disturbance: rhinophobia, or "the dread of ever having any cash."

Customers who suffer from rhinophobia always have as many securities as possible. When they sell out stocks at a profit they hasten to fill the void in their accounts with other stocks. The odd part is that they are frequently economical souls who do not believe in frittering away their money on food and drink and momentary pleasure. If they play bridge of an evening for a quarter of a cent and lose $17, they are liable to go home in a pretty depressed state of mind. Perhaps on the same day a slight weakness in the market reduced their equity $500, but that doesn't trouble them much; they still have their beloved stocks. It is practically axiomatic for these men that every time the stock market goes bust, so do they.

To them, having a sizable cash balance in an account for any length of time is unbearable. Suppose stocks should go way up? They would be left high and dry with nothing but some dirty old money.

Churning Money as a Career

Where do all the customers, from time immemorial, come from? Perhaps I have made it seem that it is no fun being a customer. Financially, over a period of years and taking averages, it is not. The statistics that have been gathered on this subject show that clearly enough.

But man cannot live by bread alone. There are other attractions to being a customer, which, for want of a better name, we shall have to call spiritual values. They arise from the following circumstances:

Our society suffers dreadfully from the fact that there are so few of us who, in ourselves, have services or talents that we can sell for as much as a hundred dollars a week. A good salesman, or a superb acrobat, for instance, can earn this easily enough. But few have such abilities to offer.

A man who has a real chunk of capital, though, $25,000 or a quarter million, expects that with this capital, plus his brains and efforts, he should command this income and a good deal more. He is quite willing to "work"; in fact, he insists on it. Only by "working," by being in business, can he assume his dignity in the world. Only in this way will his counsels have some weight with the boys at the club, and he will have something to tell his wife when he gets home in the evening. There is nothing to scoff at in this; these values are as needful as groceries.

I have set the word "work" in inverted commas to distinguish such an enterprise from "a job of work." A job of work means earning a living by being a linotyper, or an iron puddler, or a floorwalker, or a detective. It rarely appeals to a man who has capital, and I for one can see his point.

A man of capital becomes a proprietor or a partner in a business enterprise where his capital is needed. Perhaps his services are also needed; whether they are or not he will insist on supplying them. All such enterprises, from manufacturing brassières to under-

83

writing marine insurance, are speculative. That is to say, his own efforts will account for much of his success or failure, but the economic circumstances into which he runs will account for more. His capital is used in one way or the other to finance the purchase of some sort of goods. Then he performs some sort of service to the goods and looks around for a buyer, and a reasonable profit. But if, while he is industriously engaged in all this, the price of these goods bounces up, he will make a huge profit; if down, a large loss. Although he is at all times engaged in a thrilling speculation, he does not so much seem to be, because all day long he is busy as a beaver, "working."

Now an active Wall Street customer is frequently a man of capital, who, like his friend uptown, also wishes his capital to return him a goodly income. He too is willing and eager to be a man of affairs. So he becomes a stock customer. Like his friend uptown he speaks crisply and esoterically over telephones—he worries just as much or more—and sometimes he even attends conferences. He differs from his friend uptown only because he omits a couple of steps.

For one thing, he does not have to learn, or half learn, the technical complexities of a business. Almost anyone in a few weeks can learn how to put in orders, and limit them, and "stop" them, and all the fascinating patois that goes with it.

The stock customer, too, uses his capital to buy goods which he hopes to turn over at a reasonable profit. He purchases, let us say, 100 shares of American Telephone and Telegraph. Only, in his case, he omits going through the busy motions of doing some service to it during the time he holds it. He neither refines it, nor retails it, nor sews buttonholes in it. He just hopes that the market for these goods will soon rise, which is pretty much what the uptown man is doing also.

Is there so much to choose, ethically or economically, between the "legitimate" business entrepreneur and the stock-market customer? Neither of them is willing to invest his capital at three per cent, stay home, and take up a hobby. The figures on business enterprises are difficult to interpret fairly, as are those on the fate of customers' accounts. But they both suggest strongly that staying home, away from any sort of an office, has, since the turn of the century, been the shrewd thing for a man of means to do. But it was a dull life.

The man who chooses to take his money and churn it furiously, either below or above Chambers Street, cannot in any way predict his fate, save for a single assurance. So long as any of the money still clings to the sides of the churn, he will not be bored.

CHAPTER FOUR

Investment Trusts—
Promises and Performance

T HE BASIC IDEA OF IN-
vestment trusts † is little short of perfect. But as we
all know too well, in actual practice American investment trusts have varied between the disappointing
and the catastrophic. The whole subject makes an interesting study of the generous gap between theoretic
promise and practical fulfillment. Or, as George Ade
wrote of the golfer who took a complete course of
lessons, "Finally his form became perfect, but his

---

† "Investment trust" is an unhappy name. These companies
are not "trusts," and "trust" is a baleful word anyway, in finance.
It would be better if they could be renamed something like "investment companies" or "group investments," in the interests of
both accuracy and propaganda.

score had to be taken out after each round and buried."

The basic idea is familiar: the average individual is incapable of handling his own financial destiny—a fact which he can easily verify for himself in the course of one lifetime. What is worse, he cannot, unless he is very rich, purchase the best financial advice. (We are assuming for the moment that there is such a thing as the best financial advice.)

So a lot of us who clearly are not magicians pool our money and hire a set of professional experts to do the guessing. They may not be quite magicians but they have everything that should be necessary—experience, reputation, trained staffs, inside information, and unlimited resources for research. Since the amount we pool together is often in the neighborhood of a hundred million dollars, we can afford to pay them fortunes for their ability. Paying them fortunes will be a great bargain for us, provided only that they come across with the ability.

One would think they could do this, or at least do it better than we could. If they are approached with a

88

proposition to buy stock in some potash deposits, they don't have to take somebody's word for it at fourth hand as you and I do. They send mining engineers out to Colorado to take a good look. They send someone else out in another direction to investigate the demand for potash.

Or perhaps they are considering investing in a huge public-utility corporation which has many subsidiaries which in turn have sub-subsidiaries which have sub-sub-subsidiaries, until its corporate structure resembles the family tree of the Forsytes. When you or I try to peer into this situation all we get out of it is spots before the eyes. But the investment trust has a lot of Phi Beta Kappas † who can figure it all out as easy

---

† Here is a provocative sidelight on our Higher Education. Endowed colleges and universities have a large and continuous investment prcblem. Do they avail themselves of the advice of the professors who are teaching economics to the students? Certainly not. They don't even ask for it, so no one knows for sure what would happen if they did. The matter is put into the hands of certain hardheaded trustees and alumni. What happens? The years go by—plenty of the bonds default—and the hardheaded trustees tell Prexy to get out and hustle up some more endowments.

as π. And if there should be anything they don't understand they can just pick up the phone and call D. H. Muckamuck, the president of the public-utility corporation, on long distance. Mr. Muckamuck will talk. This inquiry will go through his protective layers of secretaries like a hot beebee shot through a tub of butter.

Stop Making Your Own Mistakes

If the basic investment-trust idea is even half as sound as it appears to be, the average investor has virtually no excuse for buying any securities but investment-trust shares. The question may be put this way, using golf again: if it was very important to you to win the class B championship at your country club and the rules permitted you to hire Gene Sarazen, at a reasonable fee, to make the shots for you, wouldn't you be an egotistical fool to insist on playing the shots yourself?

This would be an airtight analogy, except for one

thing. Mr. Sarazen is superior to you and me at playing golf, and he can demonstrate this superiority every time he steps onto the first tee. But thus far in our history there has been little evidence that there exists a demonstrable skill in managing security portfolios.

I have not used the big argument the trusts use themselves—"diversification." This claim is that by buying trust shares the modest investor is not forced to "put all his eggs in one basket." This argument sounds a good deal more reasonable than it actually is. A widely diversified portfolio is not supposed to break downward in value very fast because all its "eggs" won't go bad at once. (This mechanism also prevents its value going up very fast.) But this safety device doesn't seem to work particularly well. When steel and motors take a dreadful fall, almost the entire diversified list of securities takes it right along with them. High-grade bonds may hold up all right, and "cash on hand" certainly holds up splendidly, but the trusts rarely have any large stock of either on these tragic occasions.

91

The average small investor needs a certain amount of diversification, but he can get it for himself by buying five-share lots instead of hundred-share lots. The added expense of doing his business this way is negligible. If his funds are too limited even for that procedure, the only diversification he needs is to put some of his money into life-insurance payments, some into the savings bank, and the remainder into his right-hand trouser pocket.

Where Is the Catch?

If investment trusts would only function in actuality anything like as well as they do in theory, they would be a tremendous asset to the general welfare. A man's funds are only less important to him than his health and his rights. For their protection he can respectively hire the services of a doctor and lawyer, and he can be assured of some reasonably competent assistance. For his mental problems he can hire a psychiatrist and have a fairish chance of being helped,

—and for his plumbing problems he can hire a plumber and be certain of help.

and for his plumbing problems he can hire a plumber and be certain of help. Why can't he, through the device of the investment trust, hire a little competence on the money problem?

My own guess, with which by this time the reader is perhaps too familiar, is that he can't, simply because there is practically no competence to be hired. The subject of choosing profitable financial investments does not lend itself to competence. There is almost no visible supply. If there were, it would have been discovered long ago by the larger investment trusts, because they stand ready and willing to pay any amount for it. The management contracts, which pay the managers, are usually such that the managers are generously rewarded if they produce consistently good results. Surely the managers would be only too happy to divulge their wisdom for the benefit of the trust if only they had some wisdom to divulge.

Since this explanation of why the results are disappointing is not held by many, I shall try to touch on some of the others. The chief and most popular explanation is, of course, dishonesty. There are some

financial writers who have been making a modest
living now for ten years beating a dead horse; i.e.,
continually explaining the infinite variations for thievery which arise when a group of men is in control of
the handling of millions upon millions of dollars.

Such opportunities for double-dealing must exist
in all investment trusts. All you can do is pick a management which seems to you from its record to be
honest. You are facing precisely the same problem if
you are merely the beneficiary of an estate which has
three executors—all of them your uncles—one of
whom is a lawyer, one a broker, and one a real-estate
operator. Your uncles may go bad on you too, under
the strain of this and that. They, like the trust managers, may succumb to "conflict of interest." For instance, if an investment trust is affiliated with a banking house, there is the temptation to sell to the
investment trust those securities which the banking
house gave birth to and which they find they are unable to sell to anyone else. If the trust is affiliated
with a member of the Stock Exchange, there is a temptation to trade huge amounts of stocks, to the benefit

of the commission account. *Et cetera, ad infinitum, ad nauseam,* with variations.

All this is undeniable, but I know of many investment trusts today whose honesty I consider above suspicion. (If you wish to consult me privately about this information, bring along some money.) Unfortunately, I cannot guarantee whether or not they are also bright in the head. The Securities and Exchange Commission has done valuable work in scaring the living daylights out of investment-trust managers. One should further consider this: the managers of an established trust with a fairish record have a responsible, well-paying, enviable job. It is a fairly good bet that they will not, *en masse,* succumb to the temptations of thievery. Few men become thieves out of pure devilment; rather they sidle into thievery under their own personal duress. And the hallucinations of the twenties are behind us.†

---

† There *I* go. It is to the valuelessness of this sort of pronunciamento that this whole book is inscribed. This is written in January, 1940. If we now all engage in an enjoyable but ruinous boom, the reader is entitled to one horse laugh at my expense.

There has been a deal of thoughtful, searching legislation enacted against trust abuses in recent years, and all of it favors the investor. The sad thing is that there can be no legislation against stupidity. I should not care to entrust what I like to think of as "my funds" to a smart crook—or to an honest bonehead. But if I were forced to choose, I would choose the crook. With a writ of replevin and a policeman I might be able to get back my money from the former, but all there would be for me from the latter would be a heartfelt, even a tearful, apology.

Taxes, like the poor, we have ever with us. The rate of tax on investment-trust profits is now a ripe and juicy 18 per cent†—no doubt imposed on the theory that since a corporation has no soul it really won't mind a murderous tax. So first the trust pays a tax, and then the lucky investor, when he takes his profit, pays another one on the same profit. This makes what the horse players call a tough book to beat.

---

† Not true of "open-end" trusts. They have some other problems.

An investment trust should be good and large, because this tends to make the expenses of running it a negligible percentage of the whole. But when the trust is big in size, the investing problem becomes increasingly difficult. A fifty-thousand-share position is a hard thing to buy and usually a harder one to sell. If the quotation on such a position rises twenty points in the newspaper, the trust scores up a million-dollar profit on their book value, but of course actually realizing a profit on such a block is apt to be quite a different thing.

British and Scotch investment trusts have a much better record than American. They are a great deal older, and this maturity in experience plus certain differences in national temperament and viewpoint is the likely explanation. The trusts abroad are more truly investing companies—that is, their aim is to conserve capital and produce income. But American trusts rarely are able to make up their own minds just what their aim is, and stick to it. Many American trusts have a hankering to go after income instead of capital gains. But then the American shareholder (no

Caspar Milquetoast) gets impatient. Investment-trust shares are created, among other purposes, to be sold. It is hard to sell Americans a proposition that hasn't the promise of a little zip to it.

The Hell-Paving Construction Company

Thus far we have been discussing management trusts—the kind in which a board of managers decides by reason, or something, what shall be done. "Fixed" trusts,† of the sort that were enthusiastically spawned in the late twenties, deserve a word, if only as an example of fine intentions and bad results. The basic idea in this case was to remove the factor of human fallibility, a factor which, we must all admit,

---

† The trusts now in existence which may be termed "fixed" are not fixed in the rigid fashion described here. Some of these are what are known as "special industry" trusts, the portfolio dedicated to securities of one sort exclusively, such as chemical company stocks, bank stocks, or railroad bonds. This device for investing broadly in a chosen industry seems reasonable. Whether or not it is, I will let you know authoritatively in five or ten years.

certainly needs removing. Therefore they were set up in this way: a list of the "best" securities was decided on, once and for all. These were purchased and put into the portfolio—after that no human hand was to touch them. One proviso was added. If they ever stopped paying dividends, they were then and there to be sold out. Automatically, both folly and dishonesty were banned.

The way this panned out, in case you haven't heard, was nothing short of cataclysmic. Long before the blue chips ceased to pay dividends they had gone way down. Then when they actually omitted the first dividend all these robot trusts had to try to sell them at once. To make it a trifle worse, some nasty men, who perceived what must of necessity happen, sold short just ahead of them.

The Trouble with the "Best" Securities

That plan for automatic self-destruction is now only a footnote in financial history. But the notion of selecting the "best" securities still deserves a close scrutiny. Those classes of investments considered "best" change from period to period. The pathetic fallacy is that what are thought to be the best are in truth only the most popular—the most active, the most talked of, the most boosted, and consequently, the highest in price at that time. It is very much a matter of fashion, like Eugénie hats or waxed mustaches. When crinolines were being worn, canal bonds were being bought; when the bustle was thought attractive, so were railroad and traction securities. To say that industrial common stocks were all the rage in the late 1920's would be to understate it, and *le dernier cri* for the last few years has been for government bonds and tax-exempts at prices calculated to yield something near zero per cent. Interspersed with such major fashion trends there appear at various times briefer foibles—sudden passions for "war babies," auto stocks, radio stocks, bank stocks, real-estate mortgages, convertible debentures.

Here we have the basic trouble with selecting the "best" securities for a fixed portfolio. In fact, here we have the basic trouble with all security selection for whatever purpose. Implacably, this universal habit of buying the popular securities works for bad results over a period of time. It must tend to get the buyer in nearer the top than the middle. This also applies to managed investment trusts, to insurance companies, to trust accounts, to the advice of brokers and investment counselors, and to the efforts of private individuals.

This book does not intend to take up the subject of new-issue underwriting at any length, but this is the place to point out that we also have here the basic trouble with that business. Bankers strongly prefer only to float a new issue of foreign bonds when foreign bonds in general are popular†; and the same goes for everything else from gold stocks to sewer-improvement notes. There are two simple reasons for

---

† That is how that $50,000,000 Ruritania 7 per cent External Loan Gold Notes issue was floated. No doubt you remember what happened in that case. The then Prime Minister of Ruritania took the $44,000,000 that was left after the expenses of underwriting and, in a moment of emotional excitement, gave them to a blonde. .

this: the first is that those are the only times they have a good chance to sell the securities, and the second is that those are the only times they believe in the projects themselves.

The story† is told of the trust officer of the great bank and trust company who happened to shake his pen over the stock page in the newspaper. He had his staff check and see what would have happened if stocks for the trust accounts had been chosen by ink spots instead of by experts. The result showed that this method would have resulted in much less loss than that which had actually taken place. The bank had chosen the popular securities, but the flying ink drops had at least been impartial. My only reason for questioning the literal truth of this yarn is that I doubt if a trust officer could be found who would either risk the experiment or divulge the result.

A more sober demonstration of the same sort appeared in a brochure‡ issued in 1937. In this calculation, the twenty most popular stocks and bonds

---

† *How to Lose Your Money Prudently*, by Fred C. Kelly.
‡ Compiled by Brown Brothers Harriman and Co.

on the Stock Exchange are selected at four different periods between 1901 and 1926. The selection of the most popular was made on each occasion by choosing those in which the largest volume of trading occurred in that year. Their cost at that time was figured and compared with their value at the end of 1936. The results were extremely poor, and now, three years later, it just so happens that they are a good deal poorer.

The $750,000 Bird

In the terrible panic of 1929 there was a series of emergency meetings of the board of a certain managed investment trust. Late one night, white-faced, weary, and irresolute, these men faced each other around the huge mahogany table and tried to avoid each other's eyes. All their convictions were being shattered.

Suddenly one of them spoke, quietly and firmly: "There is no telling how far this thing is going to go," he said. "Such and Such (naming one of the great blue-chip stocks of the day) is down close to two hundred from three hundred and fifty, where it was selling only two months ago. It may sound fantastic, but I believe there is a chance it may yet touch one hundred and fifty. If we could buy ten thousand shares at a hundred and fifty, don't you all think it would be the sort of bargain we may never see again? It will probably never happen, but shouldn't we be prepared if the opportunity comes?"

At his forceful suggestion courage ran about the room like a licking flame. Vigorous assents were given, and color came into wan cheeks.

"Put that down," said someone to the twenty-year-old order clerk who was present. "Buy ten thousand Such and Such at 150, order good till canceled."

The kid who was addressed obediently leaned forward to write, but as he did so he puckered his lips a little. Very low—but audibly—he gave that distinctive, rubbery sound of contempt known as "the bird."

Immediately everyone felt less confident. Somehow or other the discussion was reopened, and after a time the suggestion was abandoned. My informant on this matter has estimated that that little noise saved the trust a matter of three quarters of a million dollars, but no one ever thanked the boy, because no one ever dared to admit that he had anything to do with the decision to cancel that ruinous order.

By Way of Apology

In an effort to explain why American investment trusts have not to date lived up to their bright theoretic promise, I have thus far only listed their liabilities. This is not a fair method of debate. But I wished to spare the reader, for as long as possible, the difficulty of the country judge who said plaintively, "If both you young fellers speak how do you expect I'm going to make up my mind?"

There are a lot of things that can be said in favor of investment trusts, but they make less interesting reading than the things that can be said against them. In fairness, we should never lose sight of the fact that our trusts have led their difficult existence almost entirely during the Dreadful Decade. If they all handled themselves like monkeys, or worse, at the end of 1929, look about and try to find someone who handled himself better. Did *you?*

I can't help believing that matters are conducted on a vastly better level now than they were in the bad old days of five to fifteen years ago. Time and change have brought to today's investor in trust shares several concrete advantages. Investment managers have learned a thing or two; they couldn't very well help it. From their bath of folly the trusts are emerging cleaner and wiser. "This will be a powerful lesson to me," said the colored man who was about to be hanged. If any of the lessons were not explicit enough, we now have the S.E.C. tirelessly engaged in the inspiring work of seeing to it that investment-trust officers have periodic nervous breakdowns.

Suppose you believe that today some of your funds should be in common stocks, and you ask me the straight question, "Do you believe that a reputable investment trust will handle the selection and trading of my stocks better than I could myself?" My answer is—yes, I rather think so, though that probably is faint praise. It is now generally agreed that when you are ill it is better to call in a doctor to handle your case than to dose yourself out of a medical encyclopedia. This analogy between the science of medicine and the trading of securities is none too close, but that is the general idea. Proponents of the investment-trust principle claim that they are working their way toward a professional footing. "And high time, too!" says a voice from the gallery.

The Magical Investment Corporation

For the record, I must make a correction to the statement that all investment trusts looked like monkeys at the time of the boom and crash. The statement was only 99 and 44/100 correct.

Once upon a time there were two small trusts, managed by the late John W. Pope, which were of such stuff as dreams are made on. To be exact, the time was that impossible period in finance, 1929–1931. Everything about these companies was the opposite of all other trusts, including the fact that they made big money while the others were losing big money. Everything about the intellect and philosophy of the youthful Mr. Pope was the reverse of what I have explained a Wall Streeter must be. His statement of condition as of Dec. 31, 1930, was extremely simple. All the money was in cash and call loans, which, strangely enough, was precisely where it should have been. This statement also contained an incredible sentiment (I quote from memory), to this effect:

"It is the belief of the management of this corporation that a diversified list of carefully selected securities, held over a period of time, will *not* increase in value." (The italicized word is mine.)

His record of performance was even more startling than his principles. Frequently his trusts had only a single large position, and that would be on the short side. (Nearly all other investment trusts forbid themselves ever to take a short position.) During these periods, of course, the profits showered down, month by month, and even day by day.

John Pope came to his untimely death in 1931. He was still a very young man—a sort of Keats or Shelley of finance. It can now never be known whether his amazing record could have been sustained; whether indeed he would have continued to be, as he was then, the brilliant exception that proves the rule.

CHAPTER FIVE

The Short Seller—
He of the Black Heart

I RECALL READING A
novel about a rich man who was in everything vicious
and hateful. Among his other evil attributes the
author described how he had made his first fortune.
He had "sold stocks short during a great panic and had
thus enriched himself fabulously while hundreds of
thousands were being plunged into poverty and ruin."

This quotation expresses well enough the vague,
universal indignation at the short seller. (This indignation only exists during and after panics—during
prosperous times he receives about as much attention as do people who practice barratry. Before October, 1929, no one objected to short sellers except

their own families. The families objected to going
bankrupt.)

Vague as the general feeling is, two of its implications are quite clear. One is that being a bear raider
is something like being a usurer† or a jewel thief—
that it is an easy way to pick up a fortune provided
you are willing to be immoral. The second is that it
is socially harmful.

Before examining these two claims, I must touch
on the ancient human tendency to personify general
misfortune in some human shape. While "hundreds
of thousands are being plunged into poverty" only
the thoughtful ask, "What is happening to us?" The
popular cry is *"Who* is doing this to us?" and its satis-
fying sequel—"Just let me get my hands on him!"
The public goes raging about like an infuriated mob
with a rope. Equally they resemble the ancient boat-

---

† I should not like to give offense to the National Association
of Usurers by suggesting that any young dope can go into the
ancient profession of usury and make an easy success of it. While
usury is perhaps the soundest of gainful businesses, it requires
brains, hard work, and a strong character, if not a good one. I
have no reliable information on jewel thievery.

load of superstitious sailors looking for a Jonah to fling overboard, or a Salem town meeting deciding who was the witch that caused the cow to die.

An injured party cannot get his hands on unsound credit inflation or the law of gravitation. It is much more satisfactory, for instance, to get Mr. J. P. Morgan, the perfect personification of Wealth, down to Washington to be asked, by men of moderate means, a lot of questions he can't satisfactorily answer.

However, Mr. Morgan and the great bankers are not quite the perfect scapegoats: after all, it requires some mental strain to connect up their unwise or allegedly criminal activities with our own plight. They may have played ducks and drakes with the national credit (and everybody knows what that is, even if he can't quite explain it) or maybe it was something else they did which was even worse and even harder to understand.

Our own personal plight, however, is crystal clear. We are long, on margin, several hundred shares of Radio, and the margin is disappearing. We originally got the tip from our brother-in-law, and he got it from a Very Big Man whom he met at a clambake. That Man, big as he was, was not nearly so big as Mr. Morgan and had not ever met him or any other "robber baron" either.

But how about those short-selling fellows? Now we are getting close to home. At the very moment when we were buying that stock, hopefully and constructively, looking forward and upward toward better things, those fellows, men without bowels, were *selling* it, and they didn't even have it to sell! They were looking downward and for worse things. They thought it would go down and they helped it to go down. How unnatural! How perverse! How cynical! Why should society tolerate such men any more than those who burn down houses for the insurance?

For the Defense

I have stated the case against the short seller as passionately as I know how because that is the proper and only way to state it. The case consists 100 per cent of passion.

The old-line Wall Streeters have always defended the short sellers with an intricate oration about the short sellers' economic, and even social, function. According to them, his presence makes markets closer and steadier and he "cushions the shock" of violent declines. He begins to sound like a kindhearted lady taking baskets of goodies to the poor. He is a bear and is supposed to make a good living, and at the same time he fulfills a function that helps the bulls (who outnumber him a hundred to one and who are his opponents) to make a good living. It is a fine example of the Pollyanna double talk which is the common tongue of brokerage houses.

The bear no doubt does help to make markets somewhat "closer." (A close market is one where both buyers and sellers are able to trade at close to the same price. To hear Wall Street traders tell about it one might conclude that close markets are one of mankind's most precious blessings.) It is a little hard to prove how much closer the bears cause the markets to become, because the bears rarely enter any market that isn't pretty close and active to begin with. To sell short in a wide market is to risk "selling into a bag," and if you do that you will probably "take a terrible bath," as the boys say. During a decline, the presence of a short interest undeniably "cushions the shock" to some extent, but not enough to call itself much of a factor in the general welfare.

Mr. Justice Holmes once defended short selling more philosophically:

> ". . . Of course in a modern market contracts are not confined to sales for immediate delivery. People will endeavor to forecast the future and to make agreements according to their prophecy. Speculation of this kind by competent men is the self-adjustment of society to the probable . . ."

This case had to do with the short selling of grain, not stocks, so the citation is tossed in here more for its eloquence than its relevance.

A Different Defense

For a number of years now there has been in the making a careful tabulation of the short interest on the New York Stock Exchange. It shows how much the bears sold and how much they covered, week by week, good weeks and bad. An examination of these figures (they are available to everyone) seems to the writer to reveal the following unexciting facts. These facts, in turn, are all the defense the short sellers really need.

The first and most important point, which is a complete defense in itself but hard on the short seller's ego, is that their influence is slight. For many technical reasons, their precise mathematical participation in the market cannot be stated with any fairness,† but it is small. I should say that their influence (for both

---

† In authoritative, unreliable figures, the ratio of the total short position to the total trading in 1939 comes to 3.65 per cent, which seems to prove my point to the hilt. It doesn't really; its chief value is that it is a fine example of a phony and incomplete statistic of the type which is brandished so freely in debate. (But my dear fellow, it just happens that I have the actual figures right here with me!)

There are nearly a dozen different hidden factors which tend to invalidate that statistic as a measure of the short seller's influence. Some of them tend to show it higher, some lower, and some merely show that the problem is not accurately measurable.

(Cf. pages 10-11.)

good and evil) is a little more than a drop in the bucket and something less than a hill of beans.

This should not be surprising news. The only short sellers worthy of the name come from the ranks of that numerically small class—professional traders—and only a few of them are convinced bears. This occupation, while not evil, is indeed perverse and unnatural. Profound psychological forces always have to be overcome to sell a stock short.

Occasionally a customer is persuaded to try his hand at it. Immediately he makes his sale he becomes acutely wretched and he stays that way until he has covered, whether at a profit or a loss. For some subtle reason, the idea that he owes someone some stock he hasn't got, is insupportable. What he is accustomed to, quite as a matter of course, is owing someone some money he hasn't got. In comparison, this condition scarcely worries him at all. When he buys a stock, borrowing money casually from the broker to do it, and the stock goes down five points he is comparatively calm. But when he sells it short and it goes up $\frac{3}{4}$, he is immediately desperate. He thinks it

119

might go to 1000, although precious few stocks ever have. When he buys he never considers that it might go to zero, though that is the precise figure where a great many common stocks eventually wind up.

Added to everything else when he is short is a dim unwarranted feeling that maybe he is going to be arrested by the police. I suggest that one cause of this feeling is the deathlessness of that classic couplet:

He who sells what isn't his'n
Must buy it back or go to prison.

The above, which is not particularly good doggerel, nor particularly correct, has persisted since the days of Uncle Dan'l Drew. No speculator who hears it is ever able to forget it. Some poet should arise who would sing a convincing warning on the other side. How would this be?

He who buys what he can't pay for
Is not the man to shout "Hooray" for.

This rhymes and it is accurate, but as a terrifying couplet it doesn't seem to be so good.

THE SHORT SELLER—HE OF THE BLACK HEART

With and Without Bears

Perhaps the chief ideal of those who oppose allowing short selling is that markets shall not break downwards with violence. That this ideal shall ever be attained is as doubtful as that violent tragedy shall ever be eliminated from life itself. What is demonstrable is that the elimination of short selling certainly won't prevent these catastrophes at all. This demonstration is empirical; one needs only a glance, as below, at markets where short selling is either forbidden, impossible, hampered, or allowed, and compare what happens.

1. Dictatorships always immediately ban short selling, since it is axiomatic with them that no professional pessimists are going to be tolerated. Now whatever the reader may think of totalitarian philosophy in general, I do not think he will envy them for the condition of their security markets.

2. There has never been any short selling whatever in real estate, that great investment medium, for the reason that it is impossible to borrow it for future

delivery. But what of the stability of markets in speculative real estate? Prices frequently go away up, and then, when this movement is terminated, they go away down. In fact, it might be better pictured by saying that prices, after a real-estate boom, don't "go down" at all. They just seem to evaporate.

Such commodities as wheat or copper or pepper can be sold short, and customarily are. Their prices too break far down when a boom collapses. There is no honest way to compare these declines statistically, but I think it is observable that the declines in commodities are less disorderly than in speculative real estate.

3. Right on the floor of the New York Stock Exchange most everything that has to do with this controversy has been given a thorough tryout. Before 1933 short sellers could do what they pleased. Under that system we had ill-advised booms and murderous panics, besides other periods when nothing spectacular happened. Since that date short sellers have been so restricted in their activities that your maiden aunt couldn't really complain of their sins. The resulting

*When the market gets dull enough, some of the brokers begin to
starve. To some people, this seems a beautiful and desirable end in
itself, whatever happens to the national economy.*

phenomena have been precisely the same, save that the dull stretches are more in evidence. The dull stretches do not seem to add any useful contribution to the national economy.†

4. At any period it is easy to compare the actions of stocks which have a short interest with those that haven't. In both cases choose a stock with a respectable corporate history behind it. Inactive listed stocks have virtually no short interest, and the same is true for many important issues traded "over the counter."

In the case of a general market break, what happens? Let us call the well-known, continuously traded stock, which has a short interest, American Popularity of Delaware. (It is affectionately called "Pop" by the boys in the board room.) The other stock, of comparable rating, in which transactions are rare, is United Chamber of Music. No one dares to be short as much as a hundred shares of Chamber Music because no seller may turn up for a week. (Nor a buyer,

---

† When the market gets dull enough, some of the brokers begin to starve. To some people, this seems a beautiful and desirable end in itself, whatever happens to the national economy.

125

either.) Both stocks are quoted at 75. That is to say, Popularity is actually selling there; the last sale of Music took place at 75 day before yesterday. It is now quoted, bid and asked, 75-80.

Now comes the general market break. Its causes will be crystal clear only *after* the storm. Anyway, the ticker starts to chatter like a terrified gibbon. American Popularity starts downward with the promptness of a runner leaving his mark. It sells down to 70 and then gallantly rallies a bit, having "ticked" at most of the intermediate eighths. Chamber Music, imperturbable as a bump on a log, remains quoted 75-80.

There is an hour's lull. Then all hell breaks loose and the market "falls out of bed." "Pop," still playing most of the grace notes down the scale, breaks through 70 without even pausing to wave a hand at the stunned onlookers, and continues toward the bass clef. Finally news of the disaster gets into an uptown club, and a couple of holders of Music decide it might be a good thing to sell. They get a quote with some difficulty. It is 60-75. Since they are unwilling to sell at 60, there is still no visible action in Music, save for the altered, and unsatisfactory, quotation.

Now two or three weeks later when the firing has ceased and the market has "leveled out" it is likely you will find both stocks quietly selling at 55. In this case our sympathy goes to the holders of Music, who had such scant chances of selling. However, it is equally likely that the downward movement ceased after three days, and that three weeks later both stocks were again quietly at 75. In this case our sympathy should be extended to many quondam holders of Pop. For three days they watched it tick away the eighths and quarters, with the fascinated gaze of a bird hypnotized by a snake. At 64¾, with muttered curses from ashen lips, they took advantage of the famed marketability of American Popularity of Delaware, and sold it out.

Bear Raiding

I have purposely left for last the awful subject of bear raiding. In all discussions of short selling that are meant for public consumption, everyone, whether pro or con, agrees that bear raiding is outside the pale of decent human activity. Whether they are all sincere in their sweeping condemnation I have no way of knowing.

Bear raiding is the further ruthless slaughtering of prices by selling short at a time when they are already cruelly disorganized by actual economic calamity. That is raiding at what is considered its worst.

Other operations of the raider are somewhat more technical and less spectacular. One is the effort to depress a certain stock a few points in the hope of "touching off" some stop-loss orders. If this is accomplished, the stock would sell yet lower, at least briefly, which gives the raider a chance for profit. Even if no stop-loss orders are uncovered, the sight of declining prices on the ticker tape usually frightens some holders into selling. That at least is the bears' hypothesis.

A more extensive operation, looking for a larger profit, is to help depress stocks to the point where margin calls will be sent out. Since many of these calls will not be answered, the stocks, some twenty-four hours later, should have another sharp sinking spell. This phenomenon is so often demonstrable that possibly the word "theory" may be used in this connection.

So widespread is the condemnation of these practices at this time that one hesitates to say anything in extenuation, just as one might hesitate to say anything in favor of robbing graves. However, I will put on a bullet-proof vest and mumble the following few comments:

First it should not be forgotten that bear raiding is no easy business, whatever you may think of its ethics. In the long run, it is successful about as often as it isn't. It is just when markets are at their hopeless nadir that they sometimes flash back and reach for the stars. When that happens a small group of these pessimistic villains is suddenly engulfed and ruined. There is, of course, no Congressional investigation to find out who did that to them; no single eye is wet for them. If you still think it is an easy way to make money, get yourself a large stake and come down and try it. If you make a fortune, you can square it with yourself by giving half of your profits to the poor.

Far more important than that is this question: who suffers when the triumphant bears further push down the prices of stocks? Who loses money because of them?

The answer is: the people who have bought stocks on margin, looking for a rise. They are the people who can be sold out when their margin is gone—they are the only people who put in stop-loss orders. They hoped for a large profit. Surely they must realize that they may sustain a large loss. The bears feel that way about it when they make their gloomy commitments.

A man who borrows money to buy a common stock has no right to think of himself as a constructive social benefactor. He is just another fellow trying to be smart, or lucky, or both. Those who have hopes of living by the sword should not make too loud a fuss when they perish by the sword.

What then shall we say of the bona fide investor

whose holdings are depreciated by the short selling?

I do not believe that the investor's holdings are hurt by anything the raider does.† When the raider has finished his activities, there has been a sale and also a purchase, because he has to buy back every share he sells. Why is that any more harmful to the investor than first a purchase, then a sale?

A bona fide investor, the widow Perkins, owns, and has owned for a considerable time, 50 General Motors and 15 American Telephone. When the bear raiders, assisted by fate, or fate assisted by the bear raiders, step in and knock these securities down a dozen points in a couple of weeks, the widow Perkins does not rush downtown and sell them out. She probably didn't even hear about the catastrophe, which is just as well. The bears may be able to help depress the market price of a stock. It is not they who cut the dividends.

And then suppose the widow also owns a couple of inactive or unlisted stocks, which no one remotely

---

† I am not considering the spreading of false pessimistic rumors, which is criminal. So is the spreading of false optimistic rumors, since the S.E.C.

considers raiding? Say 10 Vulcan Detinning, 10 Alabama Great Southern ordinary, and 2 First National Bank of New York? Well, when the smoke of battle has cleared away, these three stocks will no doubt be found to have declined, proportionately, not much less or much more than the two that the bears operated in.

For those readers who are boiling with rage at these remarks about bear raiding, it is time to say that I was really only spoofing. The whole subject is academic, because for several years now the New York Stock Exchange has, by definite rules, made bear raiding impossible. You yourself have seen the wonderful results of this legislation. That is, you have seen them if you have a more powerful microscope than I have.

CHAPTER SIX

Puts, Calls, Straddles, and Gabble

I N A RECONDITE COR-
ner of Wall Street, business is done in Options, or
"papers," as they are colloquially called. The business
is not large or of great importance, but it is interesting in some of its aspects. Whether or not the option
brokers fill a crying economic need is debatable, but
at least they work and worry plenty. The common
occupational diseases of this industry are gray hairs
and laryngitis. In no other offices does such a complex
numerical gabble-gabble go on.

This rapid babel is inherent in the option business.
In an ordinary stock transaction, one party gives a
market indicating the limits at which he is willing to

do business. The other party usually counters with an indication of whether he wishes to buy or sell and with how much stock and at what price he will do business. But nothing so simple as this can occur in a trade in options. The above negotiations in an option trade merely constitute a brief introduction to the transaction, and after that six or seven other matters have to be bargained about. Since the conception of stock options originated abroad where they are still much more important than they are here, much of this rapid gabble-gabble is conducted in accents strongly tinged with Polish, Dutch, German, French, and Bronx.

When the option trader is not engaged in the gabble-gabble of trading on the telephones, he is out getting customers. This means pointing out to possible buyers of options that they are a splendid thing to buy, and pointing out to possible sellers that they are a splendid thing to sell. I have even heard them, when they are excited (and excitement is the normal state of mind of an option broker even when he is home eating his supper) present both viewpoints in

134

the same session. They believe implicitly in this paradox, which is the backbone of their business.

Thus the buyer does well, the seller does well, and it is not necessary to stress the point that the broker does well enough. Many examples can be cited showing all three of them emerging from their adventures with a profit. One wonders why the problem of unemployment cannot be solved by having the unemployed buy and sell each other options, instead of mooning around on those park benches.

What Options Are (More or Less)

Those who already have clearly in mind what are the mechanics of options may profitably skip this section. All others, by making a careful study of what follows, should be able to glean a certain amount of confusion from it. The subject, like pinochle, is not profound but it is complex. If you really want to learn about options you must take a little money and buy one. At the end of thirty or ninety days, no matter what else happens, you will have a clearer idea of its multiple possibilities than you can get here.

There are three kinds of options: calls,† puts, and straddles. To try to describe them in general terms is like describing a spiral staircase without using gestures. Let us get down to cases and illustrate with a fairly typical transaction: the buying of a certain "call." (No case can be truly typical; the variations are infinite.)

Suppose you get a hot tip that a certain stock, selling at 50, is going to have a sharp rise, and you make up your mind to speculate in it to the extent of 100 shares. The usual procedure is to procure $3000 or more, buy the stock on margin, and pray for it to go up. If it does not go up, but down, it is quite conceivable that you will lose all or much of your $3000.

But suppose instead of doing this, you ask your broker to quote the market in calls on this stock. It

† The "calls" discussed in this chapter have no connection with the "calls" for thousands of shares formerly given (not sold) to influential individuals in the hope they would successfully use their powers of persuasion, salesmanship, or manipulation (or all three) to make the stock in question sell higher.

turns out that for a mere $137.50 you can buy a call, good for 30 days at 52¾. This seems just too good to be true (it really isn't), so you do it.

How are you fixed now?

The great point is that no matter how disappointingly the stock acts, even if it sells down to zero, all you stand to lose is $137.50, which is a far cry from $3000. If it goes up, you may demand from the broker 100 shares, any time in the next 30 days, at 52¾. Then you sell the 100 shares out on the Stock Exchange at the higher price and the difference is yours, all yours, except for the commissions, plus the $137.50 you have already paid, and a few details. After that, all you have to decide is whether you should go to Florida or pay for your brother-in-law's appendicitis.

"Puts" are the opposite of calls. When you buy them you make your profit if the stock goes sharply down. Your loss is similarly limited to the price of the option, which is frequently $137.50.

"Straddles" are a put and a call bought together. They cost you more, but when you have a straddle

137

you don't care whether the stock goes up or down so long as it goes somewhere. It must of course move fairly sharply, and within the time limit, for you to profit.

I have been describing what are known as "30-day options for 'regular money,'" which means $137.50. At least equally recommended are "90-day options at the market." Under this arrangement, you might have paid say, $550 for a call, good for three months. During this period you could at any time demand from the broker 100 shares of the stock "at the market," in this case 50. You would begin to see a profit as the stock passed a price of about 56. This type of option is supposed to be an even happier medium for making money than the "regular money" kind. It is a controversy that I should not care to dip into.

I have not begun to touch upon all the fascinating opportunities for profit to which the ownership of an option is supposed to entitle you. For instance, if your call proves profitable early, the stock should be sold short and the option should not yet be called. Then if the stock goes down, you cover the short position at a profit. You still have your option with weeks left to run. Its possibilities can then be exploited all over again, like those patented shirt collars which after being used only have to be wiped off with a damp cloth. But if the stock continues upward you merely "call" for your hundred shares, deliver it, and then you must be satisfied with a single profit.

What I have thus far been describing is the use of options for sheer unadulterated speculation. What is put forward by option brokers as being the proper, or "legitimate" use, has an entirely different function—to limit speculative losses.

By this program, options are bought as a hedge against an actual position in a stock. Suppose you are long 100 shares of a stock. If you will immediately purchase a put on that stock for 100 shares, you will thereby definitely limit the amount of money you can lose in this transaction. Similarly, the theory goes, if you are short in the market you hedge by buying calls. This protection lasts for the period the option is written for—30, 60, 90 days, sometimes much longer.

139

There is no denying the fact that the above procedure supplies the speculator with definite insurance, "term" insurance, actually. But like all other forms of insurance it costs money to buy. Thus the simple question is set: is the price of the insurance commensurate with the amount of the protection attained? Unfortunately this problem cannot be solved mathematically. It can be attacked empirically, but this method of research is likely to be costly.

In Defense of the Pure Gamble

Perversely enough, it is the use of options as sheer speculation that exercises a malign fascination on this writer. I do not know of anyone else who has a good word to say for this form of gamble. However, let us compare it with the almost universally adopted method of speculation—buying (or selling short) stocks on margin.

In the first place, the option is the true "long shot" of stock gambling. A man with $1500 cannot take a

position in more than 100 shares, if that, of a moder-
ately priced stock. He can, however, buy a 30-day
option on 1000 shares if he feels sufficiently heady
about its immediate future. It is quite conceivable that
the stock will move ten points in the proper direction
in the course of a month. In this case, the option
buyer wins $10,000 for his stake and the margin
buyer only $1000 for the same stake. (The poor fel-
low who only bought as much as he could pay for
with $1500 shows a profit of less than $500.)

There is nothing particularly improbable about
that pleasant little story, but I never happened to be
around when it occurred.

My second point, oddly, is a moral one. When a
man buys an option he pays for it with his small stake,
and then if his venture is unsuccessful that money is
gone forever. Nevertheless that is *all* the money he
is going to shell out on this particular venture, come
what may. Neither his subsequent folly nor wisdom
can cause him to get involved any deeper. The margin buyer, on the other hand, frequently thinks he is
going to take a limited gamble only. Then things go

141

wrong: he gets a little hysterical (which he didn't expect to do), he puts up more money and eventually loses his patrimony (which he didn't expect to do). It is the case, quoted previously, of failing to get off the Twentieth Century Limited at 125th Street.

While I am prating in this objectionable way about morals, it is only fair to consider a popular moral objection to the gambling option buyer. "I," says the margin buyer, "am actually putting up a substantial amount of money toward the actual purchase of some stock. I am joining, in a forward-looking, constructive, patriotic sort of way, in a corporate enterprise. Your option buyer is merely making a complex wager with someone about the near future price of the stock."

A little further examination will show, however, that the functional differences between these two speculative fellow travelers is not so great. The margin buyer never sees his stock, any more than does the option buyer. He doesn't really own it; it is not registered in his name. He can arrange to be admitted to stockholders' meetings if he wants to—but he doesn't want to, nor would he accomplish anything much if he did. Both men receive dividends, if any, on the books; not into their pockets. The broker who sold the option represents someone who either has the stock, or who hustles out and buys it.

The Catch

It would be monstrous to leave an impressionable reader with the idea that the buying of options is a reliable way to make money. But the practice has so few spokesmen that I have taken it on myself to suggest that it has at least as much to recommend it as more approved speculative methods.

Options are infinitely attractive to dream about. We all know many stocks which have moved much more than ten points in a month, and more than fifty points in three months. But when a man stops dreaming these transactions and tries doing them, something different always seems to happen.

The customer who buys some options soon discov-

143

ers that his costs are considerably higher than at first appears. Commissions, stamps, and disappointing executions on the floor all hamper him. These, however, are only details.

Choosing the proper stock, at the proper time, for the proper move, is difficult. But the greatest difficulty, I am grieved to report, arises after that has all been successfully done.

Option brokers are fond of pointing out all the advantageous ways there are of "operating" once the option "gets into the money." It is indeed the truth; one can do more fascinating things with an option than an inventive boy can do with a set of Meccano. But for some subtle reason, whatever one does at this point usually turns out to be wrong.

For instance, suppose we have a profit of three points after one week has elapsed of a 30-day call on 100 shares. Shall we do the simplest thing, which is to do nothing, and wait for the big ten-point rise? Maybe, but perhaps the stock will go down again, never to rally, and then our chance for profit is gone forever. Well, then, shall we sell 100 shares short?

144

It is indeed the truth; one can do more fascinating things with an option than an inventive boy can do with a set of Meccano.

Then if the stock continues up we shall only have a profit of $300 when we could have had $1000, which is what we originally had in mind, dopes that we are! Or shall we sell 50 shares short? That is attractive; that will get us some more profit whichever way the stock moves. But it will get us only one half the possible profit, so we don't much care to do that.

Thus what usually happens on those infrequent occasions when we have chosen the right stock at the right time is that we end up with a picayune profit, if any, plus a nice foundation for a set of stomach ulcers.

In conclusion, I leave you with this suggestion. The next time you get a hot, fast tip, quote the option market. I do not say that you should necessarily buy a call. But you should at least mull over for a little the fact that there exists a group of gentlemen who seem willing to wager that this stock is not going to go so very high in the next 30 or 90 days, after all.

CHAPTER SEVEN

The "Good" Old Days and the "Great" Captains

I N ATTEMPTING TO find out just what, if anything, was good in the good old days it is necessary to determine when the good old days were. In some simple, but not straightforward, Wall Street minds, they were any days that preceded the Securities and Exchange Commission, when there weren't no ten commandments and a man could raise a thirst. Oh for the days when the most important rules were "Don't rebate on commissions," "Don't shoot the specialists," and "Don't smoke opium on the floor during trading hours."

It would be more correct and more honest to recognize that the good old days were simply boom days, like the booms of the late twenties, the late teens, and the late nineteenth century. Come to think of it, that was a fairish little boom in '36-37, wasn't it, fellows? That time the S.E.C. was all but sitting in the game with us, joggling our elbows, breathing down the backs of our necks, and making suggestions right in the middle of the bidding. They often emptied the ash trays, but they never served any beer and sandwiches. They certainly didn't start the boom or nourish it, and I don't believe they had much to do with stopping it. Booms go boom.

In our moments of sober thought we all realize that booms are bad things, not good. But nearly all of us have a secret hankering for another one. "Another little orgy wouldn't do us any harm," is the feeling that persists both downtown and up. This is quite human, because in the last boom we acted so silly. If we are old enough we probably acted silly in the last three. We either got in too late, or out too late, or both. But now that we are experienced, just give us one more shot at a good reliable runaway boom!

149

The I.Q. of a Big Shot

There has evolved a considerable saga of the deeds and derring-do of the Great Speculators of the good old days. I shall not touch on their morals, such as they were, since that subject has been covered with completeness and passion by others. I am more interested in their mentalities, which are popularly considered to have been very high.

The men under discussion are those who made, and often lost, their fortunes in stocks, trading them, manipulating them, cornering them, and generally performing razzle-dazzle with them. This excludes such men as Rockefeller and Carnegie who were primarily engaged in such realistic businesses as oil and steel —their Wall Street interests only grew secondarily from that. But your true speculator starts near the corner of Wall and Broad and doesn't wander farther away than the next two tickers. He knows that in some savage unvisited spot like Jersey City a corporation is actually in business, but he doesn't really think that important. What fascinates him is that against this vague concept of a living business certain pieces of engraved paper can be issued, and that with these pieces of paper thrilling games can be played. He does not easily conceive the business in terms of workers, management, products, processes, markets, and patents. Much more simply he thinks of the Norfolk and Western Railroad as NFK, and the United States Steel Corporation as X. What is most clearly in his mind is that if he wants to make a play a fellow can always find a large close market in X but not in NFK.

This inability to grasp ultimate realities is the outstanding mental deficiency of the speculator, small as well as great. He is an incurable romantic and usually egotistical. His mind is fast, active, and resourceful, and, in a peculiarly limited way, shrewd. That is, he is shrewd in everything save that he is constantly, day by day, laying himself open to the possibility of being ruined. He seems to believe, with Mother Goose, that a treetop is the proper place for a cradle.

Nowhere is this lack of reality more tragic than in the speculator's failure to comprehend what money really is. He doesn't know what it is, though his stenographer does. He thinks it is an item on the right-hand side of a broker's statement. He doesn't know what it is for, though you and I do, and could easily tell him. He thinks it is for "swinging a big line" of some active common stock.

If a man makes thirty million dollars, and then loses the entire thirty million and some more to boot, would you say that such a man is quite bright in the head? I will raise no objection if a man has thirty million and, in the course of trying to amuse himself, loses twenty-nine and a half million, for in this case no real harm has been done and no sympathy need be extended. But this rarely happens. When they really begin to go, they "go" for everything they have— and some more that they haven't.

Frequently such men are given second and third and even fourth chances. They blarney their way into another big grubstake and start over. This is not so difficult as it might seem to you and me. The feeling in Wall Street is that a man whose business record consists in having made thirty millions and lost thirty-five millions is a whale of a boy and a valuable business associate. (The funny part is that this is often true. While the net returns of his efforts over a period of time amount to a loss of five million dollars, he is, undeniably, the man who can stir things up and give a firm "action.")

I know this hardly seems fair. No one is going to set up you or me with a huge credit, and our business record is much superior to his. You and I never lost any five million dollars—no, sir, we wouldn't do such a thing. On the score, our commercial achievement is five million ahead of his, plus what we have gotten over a period of years in the weekly pay envelope. But another great advantage that he has got over us is that he owes his debtors such huge amounts. His debtors feel (possibly mistakenly) that their best chance of getting their big "marker" back is to supply him with another bank roll so that he can start operating again. Our debtors are different. They are the dentist, the tailor, and the finance company. They don't have the same conception of it at all.

I should like to carry this inquiry into intelligence

153

a little further and ask a second question: what do you think of the mentality of a man who goes down to Wall Street with very little and wins, by speculation, thirty millions, none of which he has as yet lost? My own considered opinion is that he too is pretty much of a loony. In order to make his second unimportant million he had to risk his first precious million. Obviously he did so, and did it time and again. That he happens to have been successful each time does not really change the picture. What *could* he have been thinking of each time he took all those risks? The very contemplation of it makes my bourgeois soul shudder.

It is now high time to allow the reader to ask a pertinent question. He asks with justice and some asperity, "Just what authority have you, sitting at that desk with an ink smudge on your nose, to criticize the mental qualities of a man who has made thirty million dollars?" I figure I have the same authority as the fan at the ball game who yells, "You big dope!" when the Yankee short-stop scoops up a hard grounder and throws to the wrong base. The fan

is conceded to have a right to express this sound opinion even though it is admitted that if the fan had been
in the short-stop's place he would not have stopped
the ball at all, save possibly with his Adam's apple.
Anyway, he certainly wouldn't have thrown to the
wrong base.

Speculation on Speculation

Thus far we have been inquiring as to whether
large speculation is a sensible occupation in itself. I
should now like to look into a somewhat different
matter. When they are speculating, how much of
what the speculators are doing is wisdom and fore-
sight and experience, and how much is sheer guessing? Certainly they never admit to themselves that
they are making guesses, or they would have to quit
the business at which they have so much fun. If they
are acting on guesses or hunches, as I suspect they
are, they are the world's best rationalizers in finding
profound reasons for their hunches.

Consider "tape readers," for instance. I have observed the devotees of this peculiar profession on and off for many years. They claim that the tape, worming its way out of the ticker, tells the initiate a complex story that cannot be perceived by others. Maybe so. The old-time speculators were all popularly supposed to number tape reading among their accomplishments, just as we assume that Arturo Toscanini can play the piano, though we have never seen him do it.

To me it seems that tape reading is very light reading indeed. There seems so little to read. The tape records the transactions on the floor in the order of occurrence, and shows the volume and prices at which they take place. It does not show who the buyers and sellers were, or what they were thinking of when they bought and sold, or what they intend to do next, if anything. Nor does it print anything about what is about to occur in Europe, Washington, or the dust bowl. Tape readers will reply that what I don't know about the tape will fill a large book. They feel that after years of peering at those marching prices they

have developed a "trading instinct." † I have heard
a man boast that when the market was breaking he
could tell it with his eyes closed just by *listening* to
the ticker. This feat could also be performed by your
little niece since the ticker does set up a clatter during
a break. But I don't see how either of them can fore-
tell how severe the break is going to be, or how long
it will last, even with their eyes open.

There is a well-known story of a shrewd plunger
and tape reader of the old days who received a strong
tip to buy a certain railroad stock. What he first did,
to the consternation of beholders, was to sell ten thousand shares short. But it turned out that he had in-
dulged in this expensive gesture simply to "test the
market" and determine whether the tip was sincere.
He watched the tape, observed that the market "took
his offerings in an orderly fashion," and was thus convinced. So he turned around, bought in the ten thousand he had sold, and then bought an additional fifty
thousand. In practically no time he had made a fortune.

---

† Read any psychologist on the popular misconceptions as to
what "instinct" is.

To me this anecdote has a distinctly dreamlike quality, and I note that this method of trading has not persisted into recent times. No doubt this performance did occur at least once; there was no limit to what those megalomaniacs might do. If the plunger made a common practice of this stunt I do not envy him. (But I should have liked to have been his broker.)

I do not know any way to determine authoritatively the question of how much of a speculator's activity is sheer guesswork, disguised, and how much is sensible. (Bear in mind that we are discussing speculators, not crooks. A crook's business is realistic; so long as he is effectively crooked he is not a speculator at all. What we are discussing is speculators whose actions are prompted by tape reading, chart reading, statistical analysis, inside information, trading instinct, and all of that.)

Let us toy with the notion that all of it, or nearly all of it, is actually guesswork. But this cannot be so, it is objected, because a certain few men, year in and year out, who are speculators, not crooks, make a good

158

thing of it. There are not many of them, but there
are, and always have been, a few. And they win.
Doesn't this prove that successful speculation is something more than good luck? The answer, I suspect, is
no. And this is why I suspect it.

A Brief Excursion into Probabilities

There is a mathematical demonstration of what
would happen, what *must* happen, if a large number
of men were set to playing a game of pure chance
against each other. The demonstration is interesting,
but the reader must determine for himself whether or
not it is analogous to Wall Street speculation. Here
it is:

Let us have 400,000 men (and women) engage in
this contest at one time. (Something like the number
in this country who try being speculators.) We line
them up, facing each other in pairs, across a refectory
table miles long. Each player is going to play the
person facing him a series of games, the game chosen
being a matter of pure luck, say matching coins. Two

hundred thousand on one side of the table face 200,-
000 on the other side.

If the reader is at all mathematically inclined he
should cease reading and work out for himself what
is now bound to occur. Otherwise:

The referee gives a signal for the first game and
400,000 coins flash in the sun as they are tossed. The
scorers make their tabulations, and discover that 200,-
000 people are winners and 200,000 are losers. Then
the second game is played. Of the original 200,000
winners, about half of them win again. We now have
about 100,000 who have won two games and an
equal number who have been so unfortunate as to
lose both games. The rest have so far broken even.
The simplest thing from now on is to keep our eyes
on the winners. (No one is ever much interested in
the losers, anyway.)

The third game is played, and of the 100,000 who
have won both games half of them are again successful. These 50,000, in the fourth game, are reduced to
25,000, and in the fifth to 12,500. These 12,500 have
now won five straight without a loss and are no doubt

beginning to fancy themselves as coin flippers. They feel they have an "instinct" for it. However, in the sixth game, 6250 of them are disappointed and amazed to find that they have finally lost, and perhaps some of them start a Congressional investigation. But the victorious 6250 play on and are successively reduced in number until less than a thousand are left. This little band has won some nine straight without a loss, and by this time most of them have at least a local reputation for their ability. People come from some distance to consult them about their method of calling heads and tails, and they modestly give explanations of how they have achieved their success. Eventually there are about a dozen men who have won every single time for about fifteen games. These are regarded as the experts, the greatest coin flippers in history, the men who never lose, and they have their biographies written.

Admittedly, it is preposterous to suggest that stock speculation is like coin flipping. I know that there is more skill to stock speculation. What I have never been able to determine is—how much more?

Down Will Come Baby

When a speculator is riding the crest he does indeed give a convincing appearance of infallibility. Not only are all beholders impressed, but he cannot help being impressed with himself. The deference he receives from his associates, his rivals, and the head-waiters of night clubs is a sincere and moving thing. But when he starts to toboggan down the other side of the hill, what becomes of the wisdom that was so evident a short time before? Who has gotten inside his skull and tampered with that fine brain?

Sometimes he recovers himself before hitting bottom and sometimes he doesn't. If he doesn't, there finally comes the day when the collar of his last Sulka shirt is frayed. Then he, who often found it easy to produce a couple of thousand dollars in a day, finds it dreadfully hard to earn that much in a year. Often the cycle is brief. There was that day when, without much grace, he bade farewell forever to the company of poor men. Then perhaps it was only a few years later that, with less grace, he awkwardly tries to rejoin them, and finds that they are not much interested in listening to his former exploits.

In Thackeray's *Vanity Fair* there is a masterly description of a ruined speculator, which demonstrates that the genus has not altered an iota in over a century. Old Mr. Sedley was not a realist, either. He felt strongly that that scoundrel Napoleon had escaped from Elba and rallied all France to his banner chiefly for the purpose of making it impossible for him, Mr. Sedley, to meet his obligations on contango day.

Most of the great speculators either ended their days in penury or came sickeningly close to it one or more times. An interesting exception was Hetty Green, who never took a backward step. She started rich and soon got richer, and after that she got richer and richer. But Mrs. Green was something of a realist, being both a woman and a miser. Few great speculators are either.

"They"

For the loosest use of a pronoun in the English language I nominate "they," as in the common Wall Street expressions, " 'They' are accumulating the coppers," " 'They' are taking profits," " 'They' are going to put Chrysler through par," and " 'They' won't let this market run away until after the Republicans have won the election."

Who are "they"? They are either the great speculators and manipulators, or the daemons of the nether world, or both. A generation or so ago, it seems probable that "they" had a tangible existence. They were Daniel Drew and Cornelius Vanderbilt, Jay Gould and Jim Fisk, and some other human oddities. Then the markets were small, and "they" were big; they played their fantastic games with the price of gold or the stock of the Erie Railroad (not an enviable property even then) and they made and broke their followers and each other.

But by the late 1920's the markets were huge, and "they," though often invoked, were deities of a very

164

limited power. Did Mr. Mike Meehan put Radio up, or did Radio put Mr. Meehan up? Similar questions can be asked of Mr. Cutten, Mr. Mitchell, Mr. Livermore, Mr. Durant, and the six Fisher brothers, and countless others whose names were then breathed with awe. Certainly when their respective pets started down most of them tried to halt the decline. They looked as though they were trying to stop an express train by leaning gingerly over the track and blowing smoke rings at it.

For the last ten years there haven't been any great speculators † or manipulators at all. But the use of the pronoun "they" continues unabated. It must be the daemons these days, exclusively.

---

† A possible exception is Mr. "Sell 'em Ben" Smith. He has apparently achieved a sound speculative success by disagreeing, categorically and consistently, with all the best financial opinion. During those three interminable years when the Pooh-Bahs were officially informing the citizens that the country was fundamentally sound, Mr. Smith was saying out of the corner of his mouth, "Sell 'em! They ain't worth anything." He could never have been "They."

Manipulators

So much has been written and argued about manipulation of stocks that I am reluctant to add much more. The business is based on the fairly sound hypothesis that the public is chiefly interested in buying stocks that are "going up." Thus the manipulators select a stock that they think is underpriced and that has a good story for a "tip" to go with it, and they try to see to it that it "goes up." They also spread the tip, of the truth of which they have carefully convinced themselves, and which may indeed turn out to be true.

If the manipulators make the price rise by washed sales (which are not true transactions and don't cost anything but commissions) my opinion is that this is a fraud and that a moderate stay in jail would not be out of place for them, even though personally they are jolly fellows. It is, of course, equally pernicious fraud if they spread false information to go with the washed sales, and a double sentence should be in order. But if they make the price go up by actually buy-

166

ing the stock and paying money for it, I tend to wish them luck, if for no other reason than that they are certainly going to need it.

Eor, at the conclusion of this first part of the operation they find themselves the owners of a great deal of stock, purchased at ascending prices. At this point the gullible public is supposed to come galloping in to buy the stock from the manipulators at still higher prices. But not infrequently the gullible public acts like an overfed trout and just pays no attention. When this happens the operators, who in the beginning fancied themselves as devilish manipulators, wake up one morning to find that they have become involuntary investors.

Manipulation, like other frowned-on practices I have cited, is not an easy road to fortune. I recall a correspondence of many years ago. A "pool manager," having been supplied with large funds by a "pool" of a dozen men to hoist a certain stock, was having no success whatever. He had bought plenty of stock and the stock was still down. He wrote a letter to each of the members of the pool, explaining at

167

length the hard luck he had run into and asking them each for an additional contribution of fifty thousand dollars. With this, he assured them, the chestnuts could be pulled out of the fire and a handsome profit would be substituted for an apparent loss. One of his replies read as follows:

DEAR MR. ——

Enclosed please find the check for Fifty Thousand Dollars ($50,000) which you requested in yours of the 15th. It was not really necessary for you to assume an apologetic tone. I am sure that you have done your skillful best in this matter, and I am sufficiently experienced to understand that you have encountered reverses which could not be foreseen. Trusting that our enterprise will turn out in the profitable way that you outline, I remain,

Sincerely,

—— ——

P. S. That is what I would have written, you (! ! deleted! !) if I had been sucker enough to enclose any check for $50,000.

168

A Bowl of Nickels

The good old days of the twenties are gone, no doubt forever. If this conclusion seems too tragic, ask yourself a couple of questions:

1. Are you quite sure that you would care to see *all* those people who had big money then have it again?

2. Just how grand was the grandeur that was Rome, at its grandest? †

In the later twenties there was very little poverty, at least among the white-collar and stiff-collar classes, and that was dandy. There was also very little grace, taste, or humility. We had practically attained the goal of a chicken in every pot, and were well launched toward a loftier cultural achievement. This was a hangover every Sunday morning for everyone, obtained at the country-club dance the evening before. Then, after a brisk Bromo-Seltzer, out into the great

---

† For collateral reading on this point, read Gibbon, Vol. I- Vol. V incl.

outdoors to play golf (originally a Scotch game), for fifty dollars a hole, with carry-overs.

In 1929 there was a luxurious club car which ran each week-day morning into the Pennsylvania Station. When the train stopped, the assorted millionaires who had been playing bridge, reading the paper, and comparing their fortunes, filed out of the front end of the car. Near the door there was placed a silver bowl with a quantity of nickels in it. Those who needed a nickel in change for the subway ride downtown took one. They were not expected to put anything back in exchange; this was not money—it was one of those minor conveniences like a quill toothpick for which nothing is charged. It was only five cents.

There have been many explanations of the sudden debacle of October, 1929. The explanation I prefer is that the eye of Jehovah, a wrathful god, happened to chance in October on that bowl. In sudden understandable annoyance, Jehovah kicked over the financial structure of the United States, and thus saw to it that the bowl of free nickels disappeared forever.

CHAPTER EIGHT

Investment—Many Questions
and a Few Answers

I NVESTMENT AND SPEC-
ulation are said to be two different things, and the
prudent man is advised to engage in the one and
avoid the other. This is something like explaining to
the troubled adolescent that Love and Passion are
two different things. He perceives that they are different, but they don't seem quite different enough to
clear up his problems.

Investment and speculation have been so often defined that a couple more faulty definitions should do
no harm, the science of economics having reached a
point where further confusion is impossible. Thus,

Speculation is an effort, probably unsuccessful, to turn a little money into a lot.

Investment is an effort, which should be successful, to prevent a lot of money from becoming a little.

If you take a thousand dollars down to Wall Street and attempt to run it up to $25,000 in the course of a year, you are speculating. If you take $25,000 down there and attempt to earn a thousand dollars a year with it (by buying twenty-five four per cent bonds) you are investing. The odds against your being successful in the first venture are roughly 25-1. The odds against the success of the second venture are "odds on," or something like 1-25.†

Thus the difference becomes one of degree, rather than of kind. Of course, a bond salesman never says, "Ah, come on, Mister, buy these bonds. They will yield you four per cent return and there is scarcely

---

† These "odds" are, of course, only vague approximations. But here is an attractively unfair wager if you care to make it and can find the necessary sucker: challenge an investment man to write down a list of the twenty-five safest corporate bonds he knows (each on a different corporation). The bet is that they won't all pay their interest for the next five years.

172

one chance in twenty-five that they will go bust." The salesman tries to avoid even thinking of his bonds in such ghastly terms. He prefers to base his thinking on a more orderly and conventional pattern. Thus, common stocks are speculative, preferred stocks are not nearly so speculative, debenture bonds are pretty darned safe, and mortgage bonds are safe. Unfortunately, the exceptions to this are enormous and continuous. Year after year it is demonstrated that the common stocks of some corporations are a great deal safer than the mortgage bonds of certain others.

Headaches of the Wealthy

People with money feel that they should be able to rent out their money at a modest rental to people who need it, and that there shouldn't be any real danger of the money being lost. Marxists feel that this entire procedure is perfectly disgusting. In any case, the procedure is becoming so extremely difficult that the Marxists must feel gratified.

173

The problems of safe investment seem particularly tough at the present moment. They were never really easy, though at times they seemed to be. Great family fortunes seldom last long—occasionally the heirs spend all the money; more often they lose it in the course of investing it. For instance, a century ago it must have been very easy to sell canal bonds to the most conservative type of investor. The story that went with them was cogent and reasonable. Canals were far and away the best and cheapest method of transporting goods. Commerce could not get along without them, it was difficult and costly to build competing ones, etc., etc. We all know what happened to canal bonds then, and what seems to be happening to railroad bonds now. And what is going to happen to your own good toll-bridge bonds, madam, just as soon as someone invents a device which will enable automobiles to leap over rivers?

Trust companies and investment counselors warn us that our investments, even the most conservative ones, will not take care of themselves, but that they must be constantly watched. They never said a truer

174

If it breaks badly he watches even harder; his eyes begin to bug out a little.

word, but in my case, at least, the use of the word "watch" is unfortunate. It calls to my mind the common promise of a customers' man to "watch" for you a certain stock in which you have just taken a speculative commitment. This promise he assiduously keeps. He watches every quotation of the stock on the tape, and if the stock gets weak he doesn't even go out for lunch. He munches a sandwich and continues to stare at it. If it breaks badly he watches even harder; his eyes begin to bug out a little. But the stock is not made self-conscious by his staring—it continues down. Watching is apparently more effective on kettles than on securities.

It is not known at the present time just how much more effective this is than the watching done by investment counselors. No box score is kept in the investment-counsel game and no batting averages. My own method of research was to ask a number of investment counselors how their clients were doing. They all replied that their clients were doing quite well, thank you, taking into consideration, of course, this, that, and the other. That marks the practical

177

limits of research in this field. You can't ask for the books to be thrown open for your study, because you will be told, quite rightly, that their clients' business is none of your business.

(Before going further into this subject, I had better include a note as to whom I am talking about. It must be understood that when I refer to investment counselors I am only referring to investment counselors who are investment counselors, as Gertrude Stein might put it. There are less than a hundred of these firms in existence. Unfortunately, there are also several thousand burglars extant, all of whom refer to themselves these days as investment counsel. This is not the fault of the bona fide investment counsel; it is no doubt a subtle compliment to them. Some of these other gentry allocate the funds between themselves and their clients in the ancient classic manner, i.e., at the close of the day's business they take all the money and throw it up in the air. Everything that sticks to the ceiling belongs to the clients.)

The underlying principle of the genuine investment counsel seems to be sound and important. It is a mundane one, i.e., it has to do with how the counselors are paid off. They receive a stated fee for giving advice; they do not get their pay in commissions or profits on trades, as most brokers and dealers do. Nor are they tempted to sell the client some security which they own and which, by a mischance, no one else at the moment seems to care to buy. Thus a wealthy person may at least feel sure that the advice he gets from investment counsel is sincere, and unbiased by hope of gain or fear of loss. This reduces the wealthy person's problems to two:

(1) Is there such a thing as consistently useful financial advice?
(2) If there is, which investment counselor can supply it?

In spite of the fact that the counsel's method of compensation approaches the ideal, he has some odd troubles collecting his reasonable fees. Sometimes a number of rich men will band together and send one of their number in to get and pay for the service.

179

Then they will all use it. If it surprises you that there are millionaires who will stoop to such petty chiseling you should get out and meet more millionaires. Sometimes the advice, though perhaps good, does not seem sufficiently spectacular. There was a man who took his large estate to the investment counsel and emerged looking a little dazed.

"What did they tell you to do?" asked his friend.

"They told me to sell everything and put all the money, except $3500, into government bonds."

"What did they tell you to do with the $3500?"

"They told me to give it to them."

A Little Wonderful Advice

For no fee at all I am prepared to offer to any wealthy person an investment program which will last a lifetime and will not only preserve the estate but greatly increase it. Like other great ideas, this one is simple:

When there is a stock-market boom, and everyone

180

is scrambling for common stocks, take all your common stocks and sell them. Take the proceeds and buy conservative bonds. No doubt the stocks you sold will go higher. Pay no attention to this—just wait for the depression which will come sooner or later. When this depression—or panic—becomes a national catastrophe, sell out the bonds (perhaps at a loss) and buy back the stocks. No doubt the stocks will go still lower. Again pay no attention. Wait for the next boom. Continue to repeat this operation as long as you live, and you'll have the pleasure of dying rich.

A glance at financial history will show that there never was a generation for whom this advice would not have worked splendidly. But it distresses me to report that I have never enjoyed the social acquaintance of anyone who managed to do it. It looks as easy as rolling off a log, but it isn't. The chief difficulties, of course, are psychological. It requires buying bonds when bonds are generally unpopular, and buying stocks when stocks are universally detested.

I suspect that there are actually a few people who

do something like this, even though I have never had the pleasure of meeting them. I suspect it because someone must buy the stocks that the suckers sell at those awful prices—a fact usually outside the consciousness of the public and of financial reporters. An experienced reporter's poetic account in the paper following a day of terrible panic reads this way:

> Large selling was in evidence at the opening bell and gained steadily in volume and violence throughout the morning session. At noon a rally, dishearteningly brief, took place as a result of short covering. But a new selling wave soon threw the market into utter chaos, and during the final hour equities were thrown overboard in huge lots, without regard for price or value.

The public reads the papers, and reading the foregoing, it gets the impression that on that catastrophic day everyone sold and nobody bought, except that little band of shorts (who most likely didn't exist). Of course, there is just no truth in that at all. If on that day the terrific "selling" amounted to seven million, three hundred and sixty-five thousand shares, the volume of the buying can also be calculated. In this case it was 7,365,000 shares.

Price and Value—Our Special Market Letter

At this point we shall take up the subject of Price and Value, because any financial writer who doesn't explain this knotty matter has his union card taken away from him. I shall not beat around the bush with generalities but I will step right in and analyze for you the Price, and Value, of the best-known stock in the world. This is the common stock of the United States Steel Corporation, familiarly called "Steel," "Big Steel," and "Bix X" by its many cronies.

First, as to Price, on which I happen to be well informed: I can state without fear of successful contradiction that Steel closed yesterday quoted 57⅝-58, last sale 57¾.† This Price was arrived at because at about 3 P.M. yesterday someone, maybe one of the

† Source material: this morning's paper.

specialists, maybe a lady in Brooklyn, was willing to pay 57⅝ for at least 100 shares and someone else, maybe another specialist, maybe a fat man with a wen, in Brussels, was willing to sell at 58. Goodness only knows what were the motives of these people. So you can see that the Price of U. S. Steel was determined in an extremely chancy fashion. There is only one nice thing to be said in favor of that Price—it was a very definite number and good all over the world at that time.

Now let us turn to that eternal verity, Value. We will examine the corporation's earnings which are applicable to the common stock over a period of the last ten years. My word! There are more losses than earnings! There was a period of time when not even the preferred stock earned its keep. And now they have a large bond issue out. And what will be the effects of the war? That just shows you how silly a price of 57¾ is—17¾ would be more like it, and a man ought to have his head examined who pays more than that for it in anything except Confederate money.

But, on the other hand, and notwithstanding and not so fast, there are other elements in the picture and a broader viewpoint to be considered. The steel industry is the most basic of basic industries, and the United States Steel Corporation is, and has been for forty years, a veritable giant in the field—irreproducible and unapproachable. The total of its yearly losses during the late depression is less than its earnings in any one of several profitable years prior to 1930. And it would not require much of an increase in operations for great profits again to pour forth. And what will be the effect of the war? Look at that big bond issue. How easily and on what favorable terms that financing was done! In view of these, and many other bullish factors, it is hard to see why this, the most seasoned stock known to finance, is not selling at 157¾. And who shall call us visionary to suggest 257¾? It once did a trifle better than that and looked cheap to a great many experienced people.

It is quite unnecessary for you all to crowd around in this fashion, thanking me for the above analysis of the true Value of Steel common. It really wasn't difficult. The steel business is a comprehensible one, and all facts and figures on it are published in *Iron Age*. In many other industries, such precise figuring is not possible. The analysis of a chemical company, for instance, is more difficult. After considering everything else, the investor never knows just when one of the company's scientists, working in a green eyeshade in the research laboratories, will discover how to distill vitamin V † out of discarded cellophane wrappers.

I will conclude this discussion of Price and Value with the following unimportant occurrence, circa 1928. There was at that time engaged in the bank stock business, along with an awful lot of others, a large red-necked Texan. He had brought to his profession a booming Texas voice and a calcified conscience. On this occasion he had just sold a customer twenty shares of Guarantee Trust Company stock at $760 a share at a moment when it could have been purchased anywhere else at $730. The customer, the big sorehead, had just found this out, and had called back

---

† The vitamin which must be included in the diet in order to grow a healthy goatee.

with a view toward remonstrance. The Texan cut him short. "Suh," he boomed, "you-all don't appreciate what the policy of this firm is. This-heah firm selects investments foh its clients not on a basis of Price, but of Value!"

Cash As a Long-Term Investment

For those wealthy people who have not yet found in these pages an investment program which appeals to them, here is another plan which at least has a certain originality. It was outlined to me by a bond trader one afternoon. We had been discussing the broad history of investment bonds—a depressing subject. This man had spent the last thirty years trading bonds with other people's money. His own money he had always carefully spent.

I finally said, "What a hopeless game! Tell me, Mac, what would you do if you had, today, two hundred and fifty thousand dollars of your own?"

He answered with such promptness that I could

see he had given a good deal of thought to this improbability.

"I would put it into twenty-five envelopes, in cash, of ten thousand dollars each. I would put the envelopes into a safe-deposit box. I have been told you can get a small one, such as I would need, for only six dollars a year. At the beginning of each year I would take out an envelope and I would risk not living more than twenty-five years longer. That would give me two hundred dollars a week. But since a man has to be doing something and I like gambling, I would live on a hundred a week and with the other hundred I would play the horse races. That would give me a real interest in life. Most weeks I'd live at the rate of a hundred—but occasionally at the rate of a thousand. And for an added pleasure, I could laugh at the income-tax collector."

"But the percentage against you on the horses is certainly as bad as in the market," I reminded him.

"Worse," he said cheerfully, "but playing the horses is at least fun."

Your Way of Life and the Basis Book

The "basis book," usually bound in limp black and religious in appearance, is a collection of tables by which bond men can quickly calculate precise income yields on various bond investments. A good investment adviser is supposed to run his finger across the tables to as high a yield as is "commensurate with the amount of safety required by the particular investor," and his experienced finger should stop right there, like a divining rod.

Just how far his finger should venture toward the right-hand side of the page is a matter of tremendous importance for the investor. The problem is not limited to mathematics—it invades the borders of philosophy. The investor's life, liberty, and pursuit of happiness are all at stake.

"Take care of the pennies and the dollars will take care of themselves" is better than a half-truth—about a five-eighths-truth, I should say. At least as accurate is, "Take care of the million dollars and the pennies will take care of themselves."

The British, as a race, have been engaged with the problems of capital investment for a longer period than we have, and accordingly have reached a greater maturity regarding it. Have you ever noticed that when you ask a Britisher about a man's wealth you get an answer quite different from that an American gives you? The American says, "I wouldn't be surprised if he's worth close to a million dollars." The Englishman says, "I fancy he has five thousand pounds a year." The Englishman's habitual way of speaking and thinking about wealth is of course much closer to the nub of the matter. A man's true wealth is his income, not his bank balance. There are times and places when it is better to have a hundred thousand dollars than it was to have had two hundred thousand at another time and place. (And there have been other occasions when it was better to have a cargo of potatoes, or a supply of axes and glass beads, than either sum.)

The emphasis in the investment problem is usually placed on the proper selection of securities. I suggest that the emphasis would be better placed on how the investor intends to spend his income. The initial mistakes are made in this latter department; the wrong securities are chosen largely as a result of this initial philosophic error. The peculiar investment plan of my horse-betting gentleman lacked nobility, but it did have the virtue of being modest, and hence workable, just so long as the "investor" would abide by his promises to himself.

Consider the case of a family which has, besides a modest earned income, $100,000 to invest. Just now it seems that they ought to be able to glean from this an average yield of something better than three thousand dollars a year, with reasonable safety. (No, I don't quite know what "reasonable safety" means, but all we investment men use the expression.)

Suppose the family invests the money at this rate. Their chief problem now, I suggest, is not so much to watch their investments as to watch themselves. So long as they can attune their material needs and their social dignity to that income they can retain that reasonable safety. But perhaps the time comes when the family feels they can no longer hold their heads up on the block unless little Paula goes to a fashionable finishing school. For that it will be necessary to jack up their income yield to $5500. Perhaps the family's feeling about Paula's education is unreal and unreasonable, but this is a problem more for discussion with their minister, or a psychologist, than with an investment broker.

Their investment man, however, can arrange the larger yield in a jiffy if the family asks for it. Let us suppose he arranges it. He simply sells out the conservative bonds and substitutes riskier securities. Little Paula goes off to the school with a cute wardrobe, and it is to be hoped that while there she gets jammed full of fascinating social graces. She may come to need them in all earnest, because by the time she is graduated, her marriage portion may indeed consist exclusively of social graces.

CHAPTER NINE

Reform—Some Yeas and Nays

T HE PRECEDING CHAP-
ter has no doubt suggested that the greatest of investment mistakes is in trying for too high a return with
its attendant tragic risk. Not many will deny that. But
that is only the half of it—or perhaps only the quarter of it. Our subject does not seem to admit any hundred per cent truths.

There is a reverse side to this picture which re-
flects a condition that has been particularly in evidence these last five years. This is a tendency on the
part of men in a fiduciary capacity (including trustees, executors, and lawyers) to play so safe with a
client's funds that they just don't perform any use-

ful service at all. They take the family's $100,000 and invest it at a yield that is closer to zero per cent than has ever been seen before. They tell the inquiring family to run along and play (if it can find some inexpensive game). They apparently feel that they have earned their fees by putting the money in a safe place and by refraining from stealing any of it.

An intense, and needed, reform wave has swept Wall Street in recent years, and the tendency just mentioned may be cited as one of its lesser, and less fortunate, results. The adviser who gets next to nothing in yield for his client isn't doing much for the client; he is simply avoiding responsibility for himself. He claims that he *must* duck responsibility; that he doesn't get paid much for being right, and that if he should be wrong these days, he might easily lose his reputation. He says that he might possibly even be called for by some large taciturn men wearing blue suits with brass buttons. I believe he exaggerates, but he has got a point there.

Was It Stolen or Did You Lose It?

This book has thus far skirted two juicy topics—
Wall Street crookedness and the many steps that have
been lately taken to regulate it. This should work no
hardship on the inquiring student because there are
reams of printed material on these subjects. This
book has chiefly tried to paint a picture of thousands
of erring humans, of varying degrees of good will,
solemnly engaged in the business of predicting the
unpredictable. It has been further suggested that to
this effort most of them bring a certain cockeyed sincerity.

The picture in the popular mind has always been
more sinister. The public feels that Wall Streeters are
not dunces at all; that they are crooks and scoundrels
and very clever ones at that; that they sell for millions what they know is worthless; in short, that they
are villains, not children.

Everyone interested helps to perpetuate this picture. The outsider believes it readily enough—else
how did those stuck-up Wall Streeters get so rich?

The burnt customer certainly prefers to believe that he has been robbed rather than that he has been a fool on the advice of fools. Even Wall Street men themselves tend to encourage the idea. They are ever ready to confide to you what they know of the inside dishonesty of someone else. Faced with the huge losses "investors" have suffered, their egos subconsciously suggest to them that it is better to be regarded as a Machiavelli than as one who has spent his adult life engaged in mumbo-jumbo.

The crookedness of Wall Street is in my opinion an overrated phenomenon. The hearts of Wall Street men are not more or less black than the hearts of the men in the sausage-cover game. There is probably the same percentage of malpractice, but the Wall Street depredations are more spectacular. They involve vastly greater sums, and they make more interesting reading. Best of all, they suggest to the public an excuse for the public's own folly.

The indignation school of writers never tires of pointing out the millions that are stolen in the Street. But while the millions are being stolen, the billions

The burnt customer certainly prefers to believe that he has been robbed rather than that he has been a fool on the advice of fools.

are being lost. Nothing crooked—just bad luck and bad brains met together in an effort to do something that couldn't be done in the first place.

There are, of course, plenty of ways of stealing money in Wall Street. They range from the stealing of $12.50 (an "eighth" on a hundred shares of stock) to a million dollars (four points on the underwriting of twenty-five million dollars' worth of bonds that never should have been underwritten). There are infinite variations on these themes and as the techniques and circumstances grow more complex† the rights and wrongs of the question become harder to establish.

Nobody Loves a Specialist

For example, let us try to consider a few of the moral and legal problems of the "specialist" on the floor of an Exchange. The Board of Governors,

---

† Out-and-out embezzlement (just dipping into the till for someone else's money) rarely appeals to the dishonest Wall Street mind. Too simple, probably.

the Securities and Exchange Commission, and others have been considering them for years now. However, there are some ethical complexities here that would baffle an investigating committee headed by Socrates and St. Thomas Aquinas. The involvements concern what a specialist must and must not do, and when he must and must not do it.

The specialist, as you know, is the man who keeps the "book" in a stock. On the left-hand page of his book he enters the buy orders that are placed with him, and on the right-hand page the sell orders. Whenever the orders of a buyer and a seller come together he executes the transaction and collects a commission for doing it. This part of his duties is quite all right, and perhaps a machine could be invented to do the same thing.

But the specialist also steps in sometimes and buys or sells for his own account, risking his own money. Everyone agrees that he has to do this, *when it is necessary*. If he didn't, many of the executions would be shocking; they would be sometimes points away from the last sale. Thus the effort has been to formulate fair rules which would show when his action was "necessary" and when it was larcenous. The result has been a discouraging welter of legislation, hard to understand and harder to apply. Many specialists feel that what the verbiage actually boils down to is this: the specialist is expected to use his own orders to help maintain an orderly market. But, while performing this public benefaction, he is told, in effect, to be mighty careful that he doesn't make much money for himself. (There will be no objection if he loses much money for himself.)

I have before me an extreme sample of a specialist's problems. It is a sober account of a dramatic occurrence (much more dramatic than the usual dilemmas of a specialist) of October 19, 1937. The opening of the Exchange on that day was one of those terrible things which (because of careful regulation) we are not supposed to have any more. At the opening bell, prices were slaughtered and all sorts of incredible things happened, but one of the prize transactions seems to have been executed by the specialist in Nash Kelvinator stock. He bid five dollars a share,

201

though on the previous day the stock had sold at an average of 11. He bought 8300 shares at the opening transaction at 5, and did not reoffer any stock in the market for twenty-three minutes, although in part of that time the market had rallied strongly. He probably made his first sales around 8, and next day the stock was back where it had been the previous day, at 11. For these interesting activities, the Board of Governors of the New York Stock Exchange suspended him for three months. This gives rise, in order, to the following four Thoughts:

(1) My Goodness—such goings-on! Turn the rascal out!

(2) So they suspended him for ninety days, did they? That seems to have been a Daniel come to judgment. A man who has made $30,000 or more, most of it in twenty-three minutes, would naturally like to take the wife and kiddies somewhere for three months, rest up, and spend some of it.

(3) But just *what* did they "punish" him for? For only bidding five dollars? Things looked frightful at ten o'clock that morning. Would the Board of Gov-

ernors have bid six dollars? Would they even have bid four? Would the S.E.C. have bid three? Would you, dear reader, even have bid one? You only had a very short time to make up your mind, and incidentally, did you happen to have $8300 in October, 1937?

Or perhaps the emphasis in the accusation was placed upon the fact that he failed to reoffer the stock for twenty-three minutes in a rising market. This may be a sounder accusation, though twenty-three minutes hardly seems an excessively long time to hold on to a purchase. This writer is unable to arrive at any really sensible judgment on this point. The only standard of criticism we seem to have is that he made too much money for so short a time. We may conclude, loosely, that the "punishment" fitted the "crime."

(4) If, at any time during the next fateful twenty-three minutes, the market had broken further, and Nash Kelvinator stock had sold down to two dollars a share, would anyone have thought of punishing him for *losing* $30,000?

Horizons and Limits of Regulation

All reform, as Lincoln Steffens has brilliantly demonstrated, is in at least some respect disappointing. I recall a needed bit of effective moral uplift that the Stock Exchange authorities themselves successfully enacted before the S.E.C. was established. They put an end, once and for all, to the ancient "envelope racket." This was a system of unofficial rebates or of small-time bribery, whichever way you cared to regard it. Certain employees have in their jurisdiction the handing out of commission business to other brokers. They are supposed to decide these allotments on the basis of efficient service. Some of them, from time immemorial, had decided on the basis of the "envelope"—which was a plain envelope with cash in it. These envelopes were more or less surreptitiously handed out to them each week by the firms that got the business.

The Stock Exchange decided to remove this mote from its own eye, and proceeded to do so, with complete effectiveness. The reform was in every way a

204

necessary one, but even at that it was still possible for an intimate spectator to observe some social consequences which could be regretted. It was a bad year, and most of the employees in question were getting meager salaries outside of this petty larceny. The envelopes contained cash, and the clerks who received them could, if they were so minded, use the cash to get the children's teeth fixed. But with envelopes taboo, "entertainment" took their place. At that period the only known way to entertain an order clerk was to take him on a tour of the West Forties which kept both entertainer and entertainee up all night. Indeed, no entertainment was considered to have tapped the fullness of bonhomie until one or the other of the celebrants had lapsed into delicious unconsciousness in the ultimate taxicab. The money that was not received for the kiddies' teeth eventually had to be expended anyway to lash down Papa's kidneys to keep them from floating away.

The purposes of the S.E.C. are much broader and more important than such small matters as that. Although the official dedication is stated differently, the

Commission was called into being by an angry populace. This populace was extremely sore, and it wanted
something to be done to prevent so many of our citizens from losing so much of their money in Wall
Street. (There have always been other agencies, more
or less fitfully trying to prevent our citizens from
losing their money in other fields—such as the race
track, the crap table, gold bricks, real estate, and their
own unsuccessful commercial ventures.) It is all part
of a human, decent impulse which is pretty hopeless.
It is an effort to put a little truth into the falsest text
in the language: "God tempereth the wind to the
shorn lamb." † He doesn't, you know. Look about you.

I do not believe that the majority of Wall Streeters, if they actually were presented with the chance,
would wish to see a return of the good old bad old
days. This majority, which have consciences (just as
you have, believe it or not), are screaming like souls
in purgatory. But I think what they are screaming
about is the way the details of reform work out,

---

† There is no blasphemy here. That text is not out of Holy
Writ. It is from *A Sentimental Journey*, by Laurence Sterne.

rather than the initial principle. It is a long, involved subject; I am only making an effort here, by touching on a few of many matters, to point up some of the discrepancies between what is hopefully planned (and perhaps occasionally insincerely planned), and what happens.

It is hard to get a proper critique of the S.E.C. My view, for instance, must be somewhat biased because I have been, and still am, connected with Wall Street. But the view of someone from the Corn Belt is not going to be very useful either. I have at times fancied that I detected in the S.E.C. a spirit of gleeful vengeance, which should not be the attitude of a regulatory body. A police force is supposed to keep a city orderly. Destroying the city is not among its duties.

It has been a long time now since I have observed an honest broker stealing his customary eighth, or a banker his customary million. This is the result of splendid work; and it is high time the country had an authorized body capable of accomplishing such work. But I find myself wishing that the Commission would perform its functions with a little less zip and hurrah. Could they not model their procedure and publicity a little closer to that of the Department of Weights and Measures, and a little less to that of the G-men looking for a Public Enemy?

Perhaps the most important work of the Commission has been the minute scrutiny of new issues. Nothing could be fairer than this needful reform, and it has been carried out to the letter. Wall Streeters felt that such scrutiny would make underwriting too difficult, but the Commission felt that the public deserved to know every last detail of a new bond or stock issue. The Commission has had its way for some years now. What has happened?

Well, nothing very much. In 1936–37 there was a boom on. The carefully scrutinized new issues went like hot cakes, and Wall Street's fears proved ungrounded. Then came the recession and down went everything just as in the old unregenerate days. After that bull market ended, some of the scrutinized new issues set modest records for the amount of money an investor could lose within a few weeks after subscribing to the issue.

In this connection, there is a minor point of some interest. In the days before the S.E.C., the description of a new issue commonly consisted of a couple of pages containing an inadequate balance sheet, a skimpy indication of recent earnings, and perhaps a little pep talk. This leaflet didn't begin to contain the things that an investor should know. But it did have one tremendous advantage: an investor could be persuaded to read it. Nowadays a properly registered prospectus contains everything; it is as long as this book, and duller. Just looking at it causes the intellect to shrink up into a ball of protest. I imagine the same number of people have read one of those things through as have read and finished Edmund Spenser's *Faerie Queene*.

The Securities and Exchange Commission has long bent its efforts toward the maintenance of an "orderly" market. This is praiseworthy, but they haven't achieved much in that direction. Only the dull markets have been orderly. I imagine that the Maritime Commission would like to maintain an orderly ocean. But when the heavens split and the lightnings crack, one commission is about as effective as the other, so far as maintaining orderliness is concerned.

The S.E.C. has not been loath to join the popular hue and cry against the friendless short seller. From this we have a right to deduce that they not only want an orderly market, but a market which shall forever gently rise. Of course, that conception is just plain silly, like Voltaire's suggestion that a community ought to be able to support itself by everybody taking in everybody else's washing. I have no doubt at all that the commissioners understand what makes sense and what doesn't at least as well as I do. But the majority of the public does not, and the Commission represents the public, from whom, in the last analysis, it receives its mandate. My suspicion is that the commissioners sometimes strive to please their public with regulations that they can't have much faith in themselves. It is humanly asking too much of them to say to the public, "Now just stop fretting yourselves about some of these things you don't quite understand." †

---

† These observations are not official—just amateur mind reading. The Commission has never confided to me its inner thoughts.

Indeed, one of the chief points on the agenda of the S.E.C. has been to work toward the ideal of a "completely informed investing public." This effort is in every way laudable, and progress, though necessarily slow, should be assured. However, just as a fanciful exercise in paradox, let us consider what would happen if on some miraculous dawn the entire investing public woke up to find itself "completely informed." That would certainly be the end of an orderly market, for a panic, either bull or bear, would ensue. Everybody would know whether to buy or sell, and whichever it was, everybody would try to do the same thing at once. And there would be no one to complete the other side of the trade! Orderly markets, like horse races, exist on differences of opinion.

Wall Street needed the S.E.C. just as baseball after 1919 needed Commissioner Landis. But people who are interested in baseball are more realistic than people interested in Wall Street. The fans did not expect that Judge Landis would do more for the game than keep it reasonably honest. They did not expect him to improve the quality of the fielding and hitting. Nevertheless, a considerable part of the public seems to be expecting that the S.E.C. will make speculation and investment safer.

These hopeful individuals are reminiscent of the benevolent soul who said at the beginning of the poker game, "Now, boys, if we all play carefully we can all win a little."

Inconclusions

The customary construction of a didactic book is for the author first to explain, as realistically as he can, the circumstances and problems of his subject. Then at the end there is a section, something like the Answers in an algebra book, entitled, "A Constructive Program," or "Whither, Whither?" The interested reader can scarcely wait to get to this section which will settle once and for all what The Administration should do next, or what is the Good Life. The notion, a debatable one, is that the man who knows the problems necessarily knows the answers.

This book has not been successful if it has not suggested some big-league problems, such as:

(1) Should our financial machinery be scrapped?
(2) Should it be further tinkered with, and if so, how much further?
(3) Is capitalism doomed?
(4) What active stock selling under five dollars looks hot just now for a quick turn to pay for the Buick the wife just bought?

There isn't an assistant instructor in economics in any faculty who can't answer these and similar questions rapidly and categorically, and if that is not enough there are a million laymen eager to do so. So I don't feel that my vote is much needed.

For the record, and if anyone cares, I will state that I have a sneaking fondness for that wretched old hag, the capitalistic system, after watching the performance of her temperamental younger rivals. I believe we had better preserve our financial machinery even with much of the nonsense still adhering to it. The way we have been brought up, we all have a fondness for articles which can only be made in plants

213

costing millions of dollars. Few of these articles can be produced by a fellow and his uncle working behind the garage. The only successful method so far devised for getting millions out of the public, for enterprises both good and bad, is some system similar to the devious mechanisms of Wall Street. (Money has occasionally been raised from the public by smacking the citizens with the broad side of a saber, but the results of this were always less than satisfactory.)

On Problem (2) I do not choose to commit myself with any lucidity. But I am willing to submit an idea to the Securities and Exchange Commission that perhaps they have thought of themselves: they are in the position of a doctor who has only one patient, with no prospect of ever getting another. It would be a tactical error to kill this patient, even though a commendable scientific zeal prompts the doctor to try out his whole shelf of pharmacopoeia on him. After all, there is no real danger in this case of the patient ever becoming completely cured.

The answer to Problem (4) is being withheld for our Special Five-Star Flash. Merely clip and fill out

214

the coupon, enclose two dollars, and the name of this stock will be sent to you in a plain envelope.

In conclusion, I must remind you that I work in Wall Street and assure you that my organization is of course quite different from anything I have described here. Perhaps what you are looking for is a long-range comprehensive investment program, conservative yet liberal, which will protect you from the effects of inflation and also deflation, and which will allow you to sleep nights. In this case just stop in at my office and let us recommend a program. I will see to it personally that your inquiries are referred to the Head of our Crystal-Gazing Department.

ABOUT THE AUTHOR

THE AUTHOR, when asked to say something new about himself for the fourth time, at first demurred. Then he snapped his fingers and said, "Oh, yes, there's one detail I almost forgot."

Mr. Schwed then explained that if the republication of this comminatory title should happen to cause the securities markets of the world to tumble downward, he will not be so modest as to deny that it was he who did it. However, he wishes to assure all the people who might thus lose money that he is sincerely sorry.

On the other hand, if this should happen, he would like to receive the gratitude of the people who have sold stocks short. The "short interest," as he understands it, at present consists of a gentleman living in North Brattleboro. This is the same gentleman who recently moved with wife and several children from their nice frame house with the hollyhocks out in front to quarters over the delicatessen shop.